DEDICATION

TO THE 3 MEN THAT SHAPED MY LIFE

To my Dad, Wallace J. Conner, who taught me more about business than anyone else, who taught me how to be a leader, and who taught me how to give with no strings attached.

To Ron LeGrand, who introduced me to this world of Private Money, who taught me about creative financing, and who gave me my first opportunity to follow my passion of teaching and inspiring other Real Estate Investors.

To my Granddaddy, Raymond L. Simmons, who showed me how to be a servant and "fight the good fight, finish the course, and keep the faith."

CONTENTS

Acknowledgments 13

Foreword By Ron LeGrand 17

Introduction.. 19

An Incredible Journey 19

Chapter 1: Now It's Your Turn.. 27

Chapter 2: What Is Private Money? 31

    The Key To Your Dreams 33

    Why Am I A Real Estate Investor? 33

    Who Exactly Is A Private Lender? 38

Chapter 3: 3 BIG Reasons To Use Private Money?.................... 41

    BIG REASON #1: You Make The Rules 41

    BIG REASON #2: Eight Advantages Over Hard Money 42

        1.   Percent of Purchase Price 42

        2.   Interest Rate 43

        3.   Origination Fee/Points 45

        4.   Term.. 46

        5.   Extension Fee 47

        6.   Personal Credit Score... 48

        7.   Verification of Income 49

        8.   Personal Guarantees 51

    BIG REASON #3: Close Quickly.. 54

Chapter 4: My Favorite Reason To Use Private Money 57

BIG REASON #4: Get Multiple Checks Every Deal!................57

My Biggest Real Estate Investment Mistake 65

When To Use Private Money 66

Chapter 5: Why Do Private Lenders Want To Do Business
With Us? 73

Big Returns 74

A Safe And Secure Investment 75

Consistent, Known Returns 76

Chapter 6: Where—And How—To Get The Money 79

Your Warm Market 80

Step 1: Identify Your Top Potential Private Lenders 82

Step 2: Have A Conversation 83

Step 3: Give Them My Stress-Free Investing CD 84

Step 4: Follow Up With A One-On-One Appointment 86

Step 5: Ask For And Receive The Verbal Commitment 86

Bonus Step: Cash The Checks And Have Some Fun! 87

Your Cold Market 88

Proven Strategies For Getting The Word Out 91

1. Attract Millions With One Sentence 92

2. Two-on-Ones 94

3. Groups 94

4. Business Networking International (BNI) 94

5. SCORE 95

6. Referrals 95

How To Get Referrals—On Purpose 97

Chapter 7: The One-On-One Appointment 101

Your Private Money Program 102

Who Are You? 103

What Is Private Money? 103

Why Be A Private Lender?.................................. 103

How Things Work.. 103

Terms Of Endearment...................................... 104

Show Me The Money 105

Where To Find The Money Now......................... 106

Chapter 8: The Private Lender Luncheon 111

Pre-Luncheon 113

Step 1. Choose The Date And Location For Your Luncheon 113

Step 2. Put Your Guest List Together 115

Step 3. Pick Up The Phone And Call Your List 116

Step 4. Call The Invitees A Second Time 117

Step 5. Get Your Resources Together 117

The Luncheon... 118

Step 1: Welcome Your Guests.............................. 118

Step 2: Eat Up... 119

Step 3: Presentation... 119

Step 4: Wrap It Up 119

Post-Luncheon.. 120

Chapter 9: Tap Into The Power Of Self-Directed IRAs 123

Private Lender Setup 125

Step 1: Establish A Relationship With A Self-Directed
IRA Rep 125

Step 2: Private Lender Meets Self-Directed IRA Rep 126

Step 3: Authorization 126

Step 4: Get Funded 127

Find A Deal 127

Step 1: Let The Private Lender Know It's A Go!...................128

Step 2: Contact Your Real Estate Attorney..........................128

Step 3: Contact The Self-Directed IRA Rep........................129

Step 4: Email The Direction of Investment To Your Private
Lender 130

Close The Deal And Get Paid 131

Chapter 10: A Business You Can Be Proud Of............................133

Chapter 11: It's Go Time!..139

Appendix: Sample Documents 145

Sample Purchase Contract...145

Sample Promissory Note..159

Sample Deed of Trust (Mortgage) 161

Self-Directed IRA Direction of Investment Letter 165

Special Bonus Gift 169

About The Author...171

ACKNOWLEDGMENTS

WRITING THIS BOOK WAS MORE of a challenge to complete than I originally anticipated and took three times longer. However, now that you are about to read this book, the journey of completing this book makes all the work more than worth it to me. You see, I first acknowledge you for taking action to pursue your real estate investing dreams and desires. Your success is very important to me. Why? Because after investing the time and energy, I want the information in this book to make a major impact in your life and business. My desire for you is to experience exactly what I experienced when I first learned about private money, and that is to put you in control of buying any real estate that you desire and to never fear missing out on a deal because you don't have the funding.

First and foremost, my biggest "Thank you" goes to my "pillar, mainstay, and number one cheerleader," my Carol Joy. She has supported me from "day one" when I decided to launch our Real Estate Investing Training Company, The Conner Marketing Group, Inc. From answering customer calls and processing credit card orders after midnight when we launched our first webinar to agreeing to travel with me to every speaking event since 2011, my Carol Joy has been with me every step of the way. One of her many gifts is how she gives hope and encouragement to our real estate investing students with her genuine, sincere, and loving heart. Thank You, Carol Joy, for being by my side. I could not do it without you.

The completion of this book would not have been possible without my phenomenal team of editors and advisors:

Dr. Gina Guadio-Graves has been on my Marketing Team since 2014. She is known as "The Queen of JVs" and is one of the most brilliant Marketing Strategists on the planet. Thank you, Gina, for agreeing to be on the editing team and for all your invaluable marketing advice.

Have you ever met someone for the first time and "hit it off" right from the beginning? I experienced that with Chaffee-Thanh Nguyen. Chaffee and I first met at a Real Estate Seminar in 2009. He was attending as a coach, and I was a student. In 2013, I asked Chaffee to join me at my Real Estate Cashflow Conferences as the Lead Coach and Strategist to work with my students and Platinum Clients in overcoming their challenges and implementing my real estate investing strategies. Chaffee also attends and helps facilitate my MasterMind Meetings. Thank You, Chaffee, for also agreeing to put on your "editor's hat" to help me get this book ready to publish.

One of my dearest friends and "personal development coach," Coach David Price also agreed to join my team of editors. "Coach David" joined my team of coaches as "The Mindset Coach" for my Platinum Clients and joins me on the weekly "Platinum Coaching Calls." He is the creator of "The Power Within Series" and is a Certified Life Coach. Thank You, David, for helping me make a difference in so many people's lives.

I can't say enough about Brenda Smith! Brenda joined me and Carol Joy when we launched our Training Company. Brenda is involved in every aspect of our Real Estate Investing Business and our Training Company. Among the many "hats" that "Brenda-Girl" wears, one of the most valuable is "keeping me in between the ditches." Every successful company needs a "Brenda-Girl!" This key team player cares more about your checkbook than you do and keeps you from stepping on mines. Thank You, Brenda, for your unwavering loyalty and commitment to serving our thousands of students.

You've heard it said, "Birds of the same feather, flock together." Like Carol Joy and I, Crystal Mewhorter is all about serving others. When Carol Joy and I began thinking about who would be the best choice to assist us in making sure our students are held accountable to achieve their real estate investing goals, it was abundantly clear, Crystal was The Choice! Crystal and her husband, Dan, attended my Real Estate Cashflow Conference. They put into action exactly what I taught them. Their success has been phenomenal by raising millions in private money. We are proud to have Crystal on our team of coaches as she actually practices what she preaches. Crystal, thank you for sharing your "heart of gold" and helping us serve our students in such a selfless and "all giving way."

Jason Drohn joined my marketing team in 2014. Jason is the "magic behind the scenes" when it comes to managing all online marketing campaigns, including email lists, websites, Facebook and Google Campaigns, and marketing funnels. Thank you, Jason, for being a long term integral team player!

In June 2018, I launched my podcast, "Real Estate Investing with Jay Conner." Scott Paton, my podcast producer, has been in charge of producing hundreds and hundreds of Podcast Shows. Scott took me from knowing absolutely nothing about podcasting to now having hundreds of thousands of listeners. In addition, Scott helped us create and maintain our monthly membership, "The Private Money Academy." Thank you, Scott, for helping me make a difference!

When all is said and done, "it's all about serving your clients and students." Ashley Jacks is not only our marketing assistant but also makes sure our customers are served on a daily basis. Ashley is also gifted and talented when it comes to Social Media. She helps us with our "Social Presence" on various platforms. Thank You, Ashley, for your commitment to serving!

Foreword By Ron LeGrand

J AY IS ONE OF THOSE "rare breeds" that came to my Quick Start Boot Camp for the first time in January 2009. What makes him different from other attendees? He went home and put into action EXACTLY WHAT I TOLD HIM TO DO!!! He didn't try to reinvent the wheel or improve and make changes to my step-by-step methods. As a result, he raised $2,150,000 of Private Money in less than 90 Days!

Since that time, Jay has not missed out on a deal for lack of funding. In fact, within 12 months of attending my Quick Start Bootcamp, Jay netted over 7 Figures in Profits. And, has continued to have at least those results every year.

Do you want money? Do you want all the money you can get? An unlimited supply? I'm telling you right now, there's more Private Money available today than you're ever going to use. When you have private money, you're going to buy more houses. Trust me, you are. I've never seen a time where more people are trying to make more money in deals and figure out how to make money safely than right now.

I met Jay when he didn't have any private money. And now, the man you're about to learn from is the best you're going to find at raising private money. I don't know anybody better qualified to teach you where to get the money than the guy who gets money every day. It has become his life. And he teaches it. Jay is about to tell you exactly, step by step, how to get it very FAST.

In fact, he is going to show you how to make your own rules when it comes to borrowing money – you get to determine the interest rate, the frequency of payments, and all the terms. Jay is about to put you in control. And I'm going to tell you from my experience, and a lot of other folks, the hard part about getting private money is just getting started. Well now you don't have any more excuses.

Jay Conner is a player. He's not just a talker. And he has developed a very simple system for you to follow and in this book, Jay is going to teach you how to locate all the money you would ever want to fund your deals without relying on banks, mortgage companies, or institutions. You are holding in your hand the opportunity to get this information from someone who does every day exactly what they are teaching so you can do it too.

Let me introduce you to my friend, the man, the myth, the legend... of private lending... Mr. Jay Conner.

Ron LeGrand

The Quick Turn Real Estate Millionaire Maker

http://www.RonLeGrand.com

INTRODUCTION
AN INCREDIBLE JOURNEY

THERE I SAT, JUST STARING at the phone… having just heard on the other end of it, the crash, the burn, the destruction of my business, my future, and my life. It's a sound I thought I'd never hear – a sound I hope you never have to hear yourself.

Cut off by the banks with no money to fund deals I had under contract. No idea what to do. No idea where to go.

What would I do?

Where would I turn?

How would I go on?

I couldn't run my business without money, and the money had just dried up and blown away.

I sat alone, confused, and afraid.

Now, fast forward to two years later. And look at me now. There I stood, on stage in a hotel ballroom in Atlanta, Georgia, staring at a room full of go-getters; independent-minded, self-starting entrepreneurs; the present and future of the American dream; hungry, forward-looking visionaries.

What had brought all these enthusiastic high achievers to this place to hear my story and learn my secrets? What had attracted them to come, listen, and learn?

And now, what about you?

Here you sit, holding this book in your hand.

Congratulations and of course, welcome. You've now joined the literally hundreds of thousands of eager men and women from every walk of life, from coast to coast and around the world, to learn how I climbed out of the wreckage of my business. You're here now to discover how I raised over $2,000,000 in just three months to fund my real estate deals with absolutely no money from the banks. You're eager to learn how I began living the life I'd always dreamed about.

You are now part of the dreamers, the go-getters, the achievers, so welcome to the tribe!

With this book, you're going to take your first step onto the road of private money success. And when you're done reading it, you'll realize that this just isn't a book about real estate investing, mortgages, rehabbing houses, or rates of return. In fact, it's really not even a book. It's a journey – a journey of discovery, adventure, and personal growth. It's a journey to expand your horizons, overcome the mountain in front of you, and reach the top!

And in order to succeed, what you need is a plan. You need an itinerary with some specific directions. But like most people, what you'd really like is a guide. What you really want is someone who's been here before and knows the terrain, the landmarks, the destination, and, most importantly, a real flesh-and-blood human being to walk beside you and show you the way. And when you get one, what a relief! How nice is it to be joined on your journey by someone who can listen to your fears and answer your questions? How comforting is it to know that you have someone who will be there for you when the path gets confusing and the way becomes hard to find?

Well, hello there! Jay Conner, reporting for duty! In this book, I'll be your travel guide to help you achieve your dreams! I will pass on to you what you need to know to buy and sell houses using private money. I will show you the way to buying and selling as many houses as you'd like and succeed in this real estate investing world.

Whether you're completely new to the world of real estate or a seasoned veteran, what you're about to read will revolutionize the way you look at business, money, and life. I'm going to teach you how to unlock millions of investor dollars to fund your real estate deals, turn mere houses into dream homes, and, in the process, revolutionize your life through wealth and freedom that you have until now thought unreachable.

But I promised you more than a map – I promised you a real, human, personal friend, and guide. So how about this: not only am I about to share with you the complete system I personally use to buy and sell houses – I'm also going to give you access to… me!

For starters, I often give free coaching through many kinds of social media platforms. In these lively get-togethers, I cover everything you need to know to blow the roof off your real estate business and create the life you've been dreaming of. You can find me on Facebook and, of course, YouTube. I also do a weekly podcast on Apple iTunes. I'm on Amazon Prime, Roku, and more! Heck, I'm everywhere!!

I'm in so many places that I know you just want to get a hold of me, so any time you get stumped or aren't sure what to do next or just have a question about your business, just call my office at (252) 808-2927. We're always here to help! No wondering where to begin, how to proceed, or what to do next – no reason to feel alone or confused. You've got a friend and guide, with you every step of the way.

But… if you've been away on a deserted island for the past 10 years and have never heard of me, let's start with the question of just who is Jay Conner, anyway? Well, to find out, let's take a journey back into time to the year 2003…

In 2003, my wife, Carol Joy, and I purchased our first real estate investment. Since that time, we've rehabbed over 400 homes and bought and sold even more that were "pretty houses," using the subject-to strategy that didn't need rehabbing. And since 2009, we've been running and profiting a seven-figure income per year business.

We actively buy and sell real estate in our local area, do some commercial and multi-family dwelling development, and speak at dozens of events throughout the country every year. And of course, I've personally consulted with and helped over 2,000 real estate investors one-on-one. In addition, I've co-authored a best-selling book, *The New Masters of Real Estate: Getting Deals Done in the New Economy*, that hit the best-seller list on Amazon the very first day it was released.

What gives us the ability to do all this—and the freedom to enjoy plenty of time to relax and travel—is our fabulous Dream Team. Since 2011, our business has been almost entirely on automatic.

We know—and are about to show you—how to do what my dad always used to say: "Run your business; don't let it run you."

But how did I get here?

Well, I'll tell you.

I remember exactly where I was on January 19, 2009. I was sitting in my office on the phone with my banker, Sam. I had two houses under contract with earnest money tied up; I had called Sam to tell him that I needed to close on these two deals in 30 days.

He went silent on me. (That's never a good sign, by the way.)

Then Sam cleared his throat and said, "Jay, I'm sorry, but we've had to collapse your line of credit." (I'd never heard of a line of credit being collapsed, but it didn't sound good.)

I responded, "Sam, what does that mean?"

You may remember what was going on in the economy at that time: economic collapse. Major companies, like Lehman Brothers, Bear Stearns, and the big auto companies, were going bankrupt causing thousands of people to lose their jobs. Easy money loans from banks and lenders caused millions of people to be over-leveraged, resulting in a huge financial bubble, which eventually popped leaving hundreds of thousands of people in foreclosures. And of course, banks stopped lending.

Now back to Sam. After a slight pause, he replied, "Uh, Jay, the bank has just decided not to loan money out to real estate investors anymore."

Now, as we say here in eastern North Carolina, "That'll make you pucker right quick!"

My first post-pucker thought was, "Well, that sure would have been nice to know before I went and got some houses under contract with earnest money lined up and no way to fund them!" Now I'm about to lose $100,000 in potential profit on these two deals!

This quickly allowed me to understand what Dan Kennedy means when he says that the most dangerous number is business is the number one. I had one lender for my real estate deals – all my eggs were in one basket, and my basket just fell apart. You see, I'd been going about my business totally in the wrong way, but until that moment, I didn't know it.

By the way, do you know my definition of "coincidence"?

Coincidence is God's way of staying anonymous.

Less than two weeks later, by "Coincidence" (God's way of staying anonymous), I was introduced to this wonderful world of private money. I took what I learned and put it on steroids – and in the first 90 days, I raised over $2,000,000 in private money!

Now, I have my eggs in many baskets – 48 to be exact. You don't need 48 private lenders. It's nice, but not necessary, for you to run a thriving seven-figure real estate business. All you really need is three or four good ones.

I've got private lenders loaning from $25,000 to $650,000!!

But how do you find those private lenders?

How do you attract that kind of money?

I'm about to show you.

Are you ready to begin your journey of personal improvement and abundant wealth? Are you ready to go on an adventure to discover and create the life of freedom and fulfillment you've always desired?

I know you are, and so am I.

It's now time for your first step on the road to success:

Take a pen and piece of paper, write the following affirmations:

> *I Believe In Myself.*
> *I Believe In Others.*
> *Others Believe In Me.*
> *I Trust Myself.*
> *I Trust Others.*
> *Others Trust Me.*
> *I Attract Millions In Private Money,*
> *And I Have A Millionaire Mind.*

Now, you might be saying, "But Jay, I don't believe in woo-woo. I don't get into all this self-help stuff. I want practical instructions and help for a regular guy or gal like me."

I hear you. I understand. I get it.

But humor me – you're reading my book, seeking my experience and knowledge, listening to my voice.

JAY CONNER | 25

Trust me – your world is created by your thoughts and words. If you're going to take this journey and reach the destination of your dreams, it's going to take a mind primed and ready for success. So, how do we begin to create that?

On a piece of paper, write the above affirmations. Post it where you'll see it every day and make a habit to repeat them to yourself once every morning and once every night. Got it? Great!

Let's make sure everything is in order so far…

Travel plan?	Check.
Map?	Check.
Personal guide?	Check.
Mind focused and ready?	Check.

Great! Let's get going!

Get Your Private Money Event Ticket - www.JayConner.com/conference

.

CHAPTER 1

NOW IT'S YOUR TURN

WHY ARE YOU HERE? I mean, why did you decide to get and read this book?

Because, you want to acquire and enjoy a level of wealth and freedom that you've dreamed of but never been able to acquire.

And how are we—you and I—going to make that happen?

Well, I'm about to share with you the system I created and developed – the system I continue to use in my own real estate business, every day, for attracting millions of dollars in private money; finding and buying houses; turning them into beautiful, like-new homes; and cashing not one but TWO big checks every time.

Had you been at my most recent **Live Event**, on North Carolina's stunning Crystal Coast, you would have met dozens of amazing men and women just like yourself, gathered together from coast to coast and border to border, for one purpose – to learn the secrets of obtaining wealth and freedom through the magic of real estate investing with private money. Among those in attendance that day were many who were already enjoying high levels of success using my system.

I asked my students in the audience to stand if they had raised private money for their real estate investments since starting my system; About a dozen or so achievers stood at their tables. I then asked them to share the amounts they had raised.

Andrew said he had raised $431,000 in the previous month.

Cliff volunteered that he'd raised $200,000 in the past 90 days.

Carl had attracted over $1,000,000.

Peter, over $500,000 over the previous three months.

Susie had taken no training from me, other than hearing my 90-minute presentation at another event (that presentation, by the way, is the core of the book you're holding right now). After attending that session, Susie went home and immediately raised $200,000. Over the next week she was able to attract an additional $300,000, for a total of $500,000!

Kevin excitedly told the group he had been able to raise a whopping $3.5 million in the six months prior to the event. En route to the event, he received a phone call informing him that another $2,000,000 was on its way to him. Kevin had attracted, in just six months, $5.5 million dollars!

And then there's Crystal. She raised $700,000, accrued just over $1 million dollars in equity, with an average profit of $71,000 per deal since attending my event. And she's no different than you! She was a single mom with big dreams, who developed a great plan following my instructions. She has since been able to quit her job using my tools and truly change her life!

Now, it's YOUR turn!

How much money will YOU raise in one month, three months, six months?

When you put to work the principles you're about to learn in this book, the money WILL come!

Are ya excited to learn how to raise a bunch of money yet?

Now, how about a little preview of what's coming up?

In the pages to come I'm going to let you in on...

- What I mean by private money.
- Why, by using my system, you're going to be irresistible to a private lender.
- Why you need to be using private money RIGHT NOW.
- Where you can get your hands on an unlimited supply of private money.
- And all the things you can be doing with private money.

The most beautiful thing about my system—the thing I think you'll love more than anything else—is that it truly allows you to build the life you desire while at the same time serving others (very often those in desperate need of relief). If you want the life of your dreams—not just a financially rewarding business but a life of fulfillment and service to those who need it—I invite you to read on.

CHAPTER 2

WHAT IS PRIVATE MONEY?

I MAGINE IF YOU COULD RUN your business in a way that provided you with the life you've always dreamed about. Visualize your business providing relief and peace of mind to suffering people who are in over their heads. Picture yourself providing affordable housing to those who otherwise couldn't afford it or were unable to obtain credit. Sound too good to be true?

Well for most people, having such a business model is either unrealistic or flat-out impossible! They believe that the only way to succeed is to look out for number one, put yourself first, and take advantage of others to further your own interests. They think that the Golden Rule is great for church, but a surefire recipe for bankruptcy in business.

But through the magic of private money, you (and everyone you do business with) truly can have it all! Having the business of your dreams is no longer impossible! Let me show you what I mean...

Recently my real estate agent, Chris, called me and said, "Jay, you're not going to believe this – a house just hit MLS (Multiple Listing Service) that's probably worth at least $100,000 without even touching it, but they have it listed for $48,000!"

We soon discovered that the homeowner, a dear elderly lady, had been in her home for probably 40 years. She didn't want to move but was being forced by circumstances in her life to move to a retirement home. My suspicion, which was later confirmed, was that she desperately wanted to remain in her home as long as possible.

So, I offered her $55,000, all cash, and promised we could close in seven days. I knew she didn't want to move and at the time had no idea where she might be moving to, so I also offered the option of remaining in her home, rent free, for two months.

Now, what did I get out of this deal?

A home worth $100,000 for $55,000, on which I was able to make a very healthy profit, which benefited my business and me. But I was also able to do something else – I was able to provide this frightened woman more on her home than she asked for, all in cash, and within one week, when she needed it the most. And I even allowed her to stay an extra 2 months rent free, without her even asking.

When you practice consideration and thoughtfulness, really taking time to understand where the other person is coming from and what their motivation is, you can construct an offer that will appeal to what's important to them. This dear old lady had not asked to remain in the home for two months, but because I knew her situation and took the time to think about her needs, I was able to create a winning solution for me, for her, and even for the eventual buyer. But what was the vehicle that enabled such a win-win-win outcome?

THE KEY TO YOUR DREAMS

The vehicle that enabled this win-win-win outcome is Private Money. And private money is the key to your dreams as well. Whether it's building that home with the wraparound porch you've always wanted, paying cash for that sports car that's calling your name, or totally funding your children's college education, private money can help you get it. It's helped my wife, Carol Joy, and I build the business of our dreams, and we've been blessed to travel the world—including Ireland, our favorite place—all because of private money.

But private money also enables you to help fulfill the dreams of others, too! If you want a life not only of personal success, wealth, and freedom, but of significance and service in the lives of others, private money is the key.

But before I dive any deeper though, let me take a moment and just answer the following question:

WHY AM I A REAL ESTATE INVESTOR?

I got into real estate investing, by necessity, in 2003 after consumer financing was pulled from the manufactured housing industry. I had spent literally my entire life in and around real estate and the manufactured homes industry. Over a period of 24 years, my father, Wallace Conner, sold over 100,000 homes to over 100,000 families across the United States before he retired from the Manufacturing Industry in 2003. And I was there to witness it all.

The manufactured housing industry was a huge part of my life, and I would never have left it if it hadn't left me. Of course, things don't always go the way you intend them to go, and when the industry started to wither away, I needed to pursue a new path.

Fortunately, I found that path thanks to Kim and Craig, dear friends of Carol Joy's and mine. Many years before my departure from the manufactured housing industry, I watched as Kim and Craig were able to finance their dream home by flipping a house.

Kim's father, a real estate investor in Florida, came up to North Carolina to help her and Craig out. Within 90 days, they had a $25,000 profit (enough for a down payment on their home).

I remember thinking right then, "If I ever have to move on from the manufactured housing industry, I want to flip houses." And as if by coincidence, by 2003, that time had come.

That's the "how," but the "why" is another matter.

What is it that's kept me in real estate investing for all these years?

I'll tell you right now – it's NOT the money.

Lots of folks get into this business because money is their "why." They desire big houses, fancy cars, luxury vacations, and country club memberships. There's plenty of that to be had through real estate investing, but let me be clear, material possessions should never be your "why," in this or any other endeavor in life.

Now, don't get me wrong. I like the nice things in life, and there's nothing wrong with enjoying your hard-earned wealth. Even the Bible tells us to savor the fruits of our honest labor.

When you work hard to earn good money, you have every right to enjoy it. But too many people make the mistake of working hard JUST to make money and enjoy material things, which inevitably leads to an unsatisfied life.

Many years ago, when I was still in the manufactured housing business, I had a conversation with a friend of mine who was very successful in business. He was smart, hardworking, and a respected leader in our industry; he made lots of money. But one day, as we were eating lunch, he said, "Jay, why am I not satisfied? I'm making all this money. I've got boats, motorcycles, a nice house, even an airplane! Yet I'm not happy – why is that?"

The reason this very successful, very wealthy, highly regarded businessman wasn't happy is that money was his only "why." Don't let that happen to you. Stuff doesn't last. It can, and does, go away. Then what do you have?

We've got to dig deep when we ask ourselves, "Why?"

We've got to look at what's really important to us; how can we do work that gives us not only things but meaning? How does our work leave us fulfilled, as well as financially secure?

When I ponder these issues—when I ask myself, "Why am I a real estate investor?"—my honest answer is to SERVE. The greatest way to find fulfillment in life is to be live in service to other people. It's not enough to serve myself by making big money and having nice things. In order to have meaning, I must also serve my family, my friends, my church, my students, and my community.

But there's another group of people to whom I'm committed to serve: every person who's involved in every deal I do as a real estate investor.

One of the most important lessons I ever learned from my dad was a philosophy that I live by to this day, "If you are in a business transaction, it needs to be a win for all parties involved. Otherwise, you have no business being part of that deal." Later on in this book, I show you how I'm able to do that on every deal I do in my real estate business. Being able to help others win is a big win for me, and a big reason I'm a real estate investor.

The great thing is that, in this industry, there are so many ways an individual can use their skills and talents to give value and have significance. Some folks love rehabbing homes themselves, while others (like myself) enjoy getting a team together to get the job done.

I love the creative process of looking at a house and asking myself, "How can my team and I turn this distressed property into a beautiful home for someone's family to enjoy?" And I love the strategic challenge of figuring out how to successfully market myself to bring in potential private lenders.

Why am I a real estate investor? In short, because it fulfills all my passions: service, creativity, and business.

So, the big questions for you are, "What are your passions?" and "How can real estate investing help you fulfill them?" Once you've answered those questions and you want to know how to get money to fund the life you've always wanted… and get it quickly…, keep reading. I'm about to tell you how you will never miss out on a deal again for lack of funding. In this book, I'm going to teach you exactly how to attract unlimited funding – that's right… UNLIMITED!

How? I'm going to unlock the private money vault and show you how to:

- Attract funding for your deals from three different sources,
- Locate, with the push of a button, as many as 12,000 sources of private money, using my private money data feed,
- Buy properties with none of your money,
- Cash multiple checks—at least two, and sometimes three—on every transaction, and
- Get all of your rehab money up front.

See what I mean? Private money really is the key to your dreams.

If you want to purchase, rehab, and sell homes for an average of $50,000 profit or more, I'm going to show you how to use private money to do it.

Right now, Carol Joy and I are buying homes at 30-50 cents on the dollar. You can find them, too. In fact, when you attend my Private Money Academy Conference, I'm going to show you how I find all my private lenders, find all my deals, sell them all, and automate my entire business. AND, as a gift for purchasing this book, I've waived the $2,995 ticket price for you and for your guest. Simply go to https://www.JayConner.com/Conference and get yourself registered now.

But hey, did you know that private money works not only for investing in single-family homes (the types of properties I normally buy) but for other types of properties as well?

Right now, I've got a good friend sitting in a $2,000,000 office, funded entirely with private money. Many of my students are interested in commercial properties – my private money system is the way to go. Longer terms, same system.

Whether you're interested in duplexes, triplexes, quadplexes, apartment buildings, or any other kind of real estate property, this is the strategy you will use to make it happen.

And it doesn't matter where you live or what type of market you're in.

I was recently in a Mastermind group when an attendee said, "Where I live, I just can't find any deals! How can your system possibly work for me?"

The answer is because I've got 55 different ways to find houses!

Listen – I live in Carteret County, North Carolina. It's my home – the perfect place in which to live, raise a family, and go to church. But it's a target market of only 40,000 people! Our biggest town—Morehead City—has only 8,000 people. My hometown, Newport, has just 1,500. Yet I average 2-3 deals per month for an average profit of $64,000 dollars. That's $128,000-$192,000 every month!

You don't have to live in or target a big market to make big money. But it all starts with the Private Money you get from your private lenders. So let's make sure you understand who private lenders are.

Who Exactly Is A Private Lender?

A private lender is simply an individual who loans his or her personal money from either their investment capital or from their retirement account.

Private lenders make up the two markets from which you'll be attracting the funds for your deals:

1. Your Warm Market
2. Your Cold Market

The warm market is composed of people you already know and with whom you have relationships: family, friends, church members, neighbors, etc.

The cold market (also known as "existing private lenders') is made up of lenders you don't know personally but who are interested in receiving big returns on their investments.

I'm about to teach you how to maximize both markets and leverage unlimited private money for your deals. I'll give you lots more information on this throughout this book.

When a lot of people hear "private money," they think hard money and hard money brokers/lenders.

A hard money lender acts in the same capacity as a bank. He or she stands between the private lender and the real estate investor (you). The hard money lender is simply a middle man who makes the connection between one person seeking to loan private money and another person seeking to invest it.

Obviously, the hard money broker makes his or her money through the markup on the funds invested with the private lender, which simply increases the cost of doing business for you, the real estate investor. But you can avoid those costs by avoiding the hard money lender and going straight to the private money source.

Now, I have nothing at all against hard money brokers – I just don't want to borrow money from any of them. I don't have to because I have access to thousands of sources of private money, which provides me with unlimited funding for my deals.

You're about to learn how you can get your hands on all that cash for your own deals too, but first, let me share some numbers with you that you're really going to like. Let's compare in detail the advantages to you when you use my system versus using hard money.

CHAPTER 3

3 BIG REASONS TO USE PRIVATE MONEY?

As you can see from the previous section, using my Where to Get the Money Now system is a no-brainer. But I'm not finished blowing your socks off yet – I've got four more big reasons to do real estate investment with private money.

BIG REASON #1: YOU MAKE THE RULES

When you're borrowing money from the banks, they get to make all the rules. They tell you the interest rates, the payments, and the terms of the loan. But in this world of private money, we make the rules (in the warm market). You set your own terms. This works both to our benefit and that of our lenders; once again, we're making it possible for everyone to win!

For you, this means more control over the deals you make with the lender. When dealing with the banks, the banks have all the control, but with private money, you can set up quarterly, biannual, or annual payments. The vast majority of the deals that I do with private lenders do not have monthly payments. This allows more freedom and flexibility with each deal.

Many of my deals don't require interest payments for a full year. This is a big help when it comes to cash flow. But it's not just about what's best for us. I do allow the private lender to choose the frequency of interest payments. If they'd like their payments monthly, quarterly, or annually, I'm happy to oblige.

BIG REASON #2: Eight Advantages Over Hard Money

1. Percent of Purchase Price

Take a look at this chart.

	HARD MONEY	PRIVATE LENDER
Percent of Purchase Price	80%	125%

Regardless how good a deal you make on a house, with hard money there's a percentage of the purchase price advanced to you when you closed the deal.

If you're using a Hard Money Lender, the national average is 80%. This means that if you purchase a house for $100,000, you ONLY get $80,000 from the lender when you close the deal. And if you do the simple math, that means that YOU have to come up with the remaining 20% or $20,000!

That's if you are purchasing a house for $100,000. If you are purchasing a house for $200,000, then yes, that's right… you have to come up with $40,000 YOURSELF!

But notice the chart—in the right-hand column, under private lender, it says "125%"—what does that mean?

Why is it 125%?

Well, that's the average percentage of the purchase price I get every time I buy a house. In other words, I'm getting more money up front to buy the house than I need, PLUS more!

What's that "more" amount? Why of course, that's my rehab money!

When I purchase a house for $100,000, I'm actually getting $125,000 from my private lender! I'm actually getting PAID to buy that house!

$100,000 goes to the seller, and I get a CHECK for "Excess Cash To Close" for $25,000, which goes straight into my Hip National Bank (that would be my pants pocket in case you didn't catch that).

Now, of course, the house is worth way more than $125,000, and I am using that $25,000 for rehab costs, and hey, it's always nice to get paid to buy something!

Plus, I don't have to worry about where I'm getting the money for the rehab! I get it at closing! And hey, if the property allows, you can get paid 150% of the purchase price or more!

Remember, YOU set the rules! It's YOUR program!

2. INTEREST RATE

	HARD MONEY	PRIVATE LENDER
% of Purchase Price	80%	125%
Interest Rate	14%	8%

The next big advantage over hard money is the interest rate!

If you've borrowed money in the past, what interest rate did you pay?

I recently checked the average interest rate, and it's all over the board! I mean some hard money lenders charge over 20%. Crazy! But the average interest rate right now across the board is 14%.

14% is your average hard money lender rate to a real estate investor. O.k., private money right now, I pay my private lenders 8%, which is fantastic right? I mean, that's a very, very high rate of return particularly when a 12-month CD or certificate of deposit is, the last time I checked last week, like on average 0.82% for a 12-month certificate of deposit.

You can pay a private lender 8%… that's a great rate of return them, but it's not 14%, so it's great for you as well! So that's the interest rate.

Now, when we get funding from existing lenders from my private money data feed, I ask them what return they're accustomed to getting; if they say they're used to getting 4%, I don't argue.

By the way when we're speaking of interest rates, most of the time on my deals, I pay interest only. And interest only is a win-win for the private lender and for us the real estate investor – as the borrower. It helps our cash flow because interest-only payments are less per month or however often you pay them, versus principal and interest. And furthermore, the private lender prefers interest only because if you're paying principal and interest, then you're paying down part of the principal amount, which means they don't have all of their money at work on the deal. So, when you pay them interest only payments, all of their principal stays invested in the deal.

And here's a writer downer for you, so get something right now and write this down… for the private lender, the principle remains the same at cash out. In other words, they know exactly how much money they're getting back on top of your interest only payments to them.

Another thing I want to clarify here though is that as far as our relationship with a private lender goes, the private lender does not own the property, okay?

We're not talking about a joint-venture arrangement or relationship here when we're talking about private money and private lenders. The private lender acts in the same capacity as a bank.

So they're going to get the same protection as a bank or mortgage company would… i.e. the promissory note, the mortgage, the deed of trust in North Carolina and some other states, named as the mortgagee on the insurance policy, and named as an additional insured on the title policy, but the private lender does not own the property.

You or me, the real estate investor or the borrower, our entity, your land trust, your LLC, whatever or however you're doing your business, owns the property.

Makes sense? Who's liking private money better already?

Shall we continue?

3. ORIGINATION FEE/POINTS

	HARD MONEY	PRIVATE LENDER
% of Purchase Price	80%	125%
Interest Rate	14%	8%
Origination Fee/Points	4% / 4 points	0

What exactly are we talking about here?

Let's be clear, a point or an origination fee… it's just really more interest for a lender to make; it's just called something different.

Let's say the lender is charging four points—which by the way, that's the national average for hard money loans, four points—well, what that means is you're going to multiply your principal loan amount that you're borrowing times those number of points or percentage points if you will.

For example, again if you're borrowing $100,000 for the purchase of a house and you have to pay 2 points, then simple math tells you that you're going to have to pay the Lender $100,000 x 2% or $2,000.

The national average when using hard money is 4% (or 4 "points'). So for most hard money lenders, in our example, you'd have to pay them $4,000. And yes, that's on TOP of the purchase price. And you also have the obligation, and not the pleasure, of bringing that origination fee or points to the closing upfront when you buy! This means you'd actually need $104,000 at closing!

Here's the beautiful thing about private money... there are no points!!! There are no origination fees!! In the millions and millions that I've borrowed of private money, I've never paid a point, and I've never paid origination fees!!

That's right -I've been borrowing private money since 2009, and I've never paid one point. Notice that, just with interest rates and points, you're already up to 18% APR (14% Interest rate plus 4 Points = 18% APR), and we haven't even discussed extension fees.

Before we talk about extension fees though, we've got to talk about the term of the note, so that's next...

4. TERM

	HARD MONEY	PRIVATE LENDER
% of Purchase Price	80%	125%
Interest Rate	14%	8%
Origination Fee/Points	4% / 4 points	0
Term	6 - 12 Months	2 - 5 Years

The word "term" refers to the length of the note or how long you hold the loan.

Well, the length of a promissory note on most hard money loans is either six months or a year. Most of them are actually only 6 months. Well if you are using private money like me, I set my terms for between two to five years. Two years if its investment capital and five years if its retirement funds.

Notice how I said, "I set my terms…"

Remember, YOU get to make the rules! How long do you want to make your terms? Some of my students do 10-year terms! And you get to decide your own terms periods!

Let me just say that because I have so many private lenders, I keep everyone the same (2 years or 5 years)… and you may consider keeping it simple as well.

Now if you're using a hard money lender and you have not cashed out after their term of six months or a year, well, if you've made your payments on time, then most of them will extend your note. But what do they want? They want more money!! They call that an "Extension Fee." So let's talk about that next…

5. EXTENSION FEE

	HARD MONEY	PRIVATE LENDER
% of Purchase Price	80%	125%
Interest Rate	14%	8%
Origination Fee/Points	4% / 4 points	0
Term	6 - 12 months	2 - 5 years
Extension Fee	2% / 2 points	0

What's an extension fee, or what's an extension? Well, it's exactly what it sounds like. Again, if you're using a hard money lender and you have not cashed out after their term of six months or a year, because maybe you need more time for the rehab or the property just hasn't sold yet or whatever the reason, and you've been making your payments on time, then most hard money lenders will extend your note. But in order to do so, they want more money!!

They call that an "Extension Fee," and they usually charge it via "points" or again, extra interest payments. The average hard money loan extension fee right now is 2 points or 2%.

If you borrowed $100,000 and you haven't cashed out in six months (if you've got a six month note), that's 2 more points you have to pay. That's another $2,000 on top of the 14% and on top of the 4 percent (or points origination fee) that you already paid six months ago.

You now have to pay another 2% or another $2,000 in our example. So now, within your first year using hard money, you're up to 20% with hard money (14% Interest + 4% Origination Fee + 2% Extension Fee).

Using my private money system, there are no extension fees! The renewal fee is zero!

Your private money lender is going to want to extend because they don't want their money back if you haven't cashed out yet. There's no reason for the private lender to charge an extension fee because they're so happy to extend – where else can they get these kinds of returns?

I have never paid a fee to extend terms using private money, and when you use my system, you don't have to either! How cool is that?

O.k., let's move on to the next advantage over hard money, and that's your Personal Credit Score.

6. Personal Credit Score

Next, let's talk about your personal credit score!

	HARD MONEY	PRIVATE LENDER
% of Purchase Price	80%	125%
Interest Rate	14%	8%
Origination Fee/Points	4% / 4 points	0
Term	6 - 12 months	2 - 5 years
Extension Fee	2% / 2 points	0
Personal Credit Score	(check)	(X)

When you've borrowed money in the past, they've almost certainly pulled your personal credit score. Now some hard money lenders even say, "We lend based upon a percentage of the ARV of the property." And then, they still pull your credit!

With private money, that would never happen because your personal credit has nothing to do with private money.

Why?

Because it's a collateral loan (the property being the collateral), there's no reason to pull your score. It's truly based upon using the property to secure the loan – not your credit score! Every deal stands on its own, and the property protects the private lender. So, the bottom line is that you can have a mid-score of 425, which is pretty low… and it doesn't matter what your credit score is. Your credit has got absolutely nothing to do with it.

And that ties right into the next advantage over hard money loans, no verification of income!

7. VERIFICATION OF INCOME

In the world of private money, verification of income has got nothing to do with you getting the private money. Again, it's because it's a collateral loan, and it's not your personal income or your credit that's getting you to qualify for the loan. But if you've ever worked with banks and hard money lenders, they always want to verify how much money you're making. Of course, they do this with a combination of strategies, which makes no sense!

Let me tell you what I mean…

	HARD MONEY	PRIVATE LENDER
% of Purchase Price	80%	125%
Interest Rate	14%	8%
Origination Fee/Points	4% / 4 points	0
Term	6 - 12 months	2 - 5 years
Extension Fee	2% / 2 points	0
Personal Credit Score	(check)	(X)
Verification of Income	(check)	(X)

When borrowing hard money, some lenders will verify your income as a condition of the loan, and they typically do this using 2 or 3 things.

1. Your past 2 bank statements
2. Your past 2 pay stubs
3. Your past 2 years of tax returns

Now if you're an entrepreneur, think about that. Maybe you had a fantastic month and did 4 deals in 1 month, and then for the next 3 months, you didn't do anything. Now what would your past 2 bank statements look like?

It's looks like you've got NO income for the past 3 months – which of course you probably didn't! They don't consider that 4 months ago, if you averaged $65,000 profit per deal like I do, you made over $200,000… or over 4 times what the average person makes!!!

Well, how about your past 2 pay stubs?

Well, you ain't got none cause you don't work for anyone!!! Ya see what I mean?!?

And I love this one… your past 2 years of tax returns! Now who doesn't know that if you're an entrepreneur, you're taking EVERY deduction you legally can! Why? So you can LEGALLY pay less taxes.

Do you know what this does though? What it does is REDUCE your taxable income. In other words, it shows that you're making a lot LESS money than you actually brought in. As a matter of fact, some entrepreneurs have so many deductions that they show a NEGATIVE income! We call that a loss folks. Amazon.com did that for 10 years straight, even while they were making BILLIONS of dollars in sales.

So how in the world are you going to verify income if you're an entrepreneur or independent business owner?!?! Well you can't!

But with private money, you never have to verify your income! There's no reason to.

You could have a credit score of 425 (again, that's pretty low), be flat broke and without a job, and get as much private money as I do.

Again, this is because the transaction is a collateral loan – if you don't pay the private lender, the property will; they get the property if you don't pay. That way, not only are you able to maximize your profits and build the amazing life you desire, but you're looking out for others by protecting your lenders.

Are you loving this yet? Well, I guarantee that you will by the time you're done reading this book!

And speaking of guarantees, let's talk about Personal Guarantees next.

8. PERSONAL GUARANTEES

	HARD MONEY	PRIVATE LENDER
% of Purchase Price	80%	125%
Interest Rate	14%	8%

Origination Fee/Points	4% / 4 points	0
Term	6 - 12 months	2 - 5 years
Extension Fee	2% / 2 points	0
Personal Credit Score	(check)	(X)
Verification of Income	(check)	(X)
Personal Guarantees	(check)	(X)

When I was borrowing money from the banks, not only did they require collateral to secure the loan (the property), but I had to sign a personal guarantee on all my and Carol Joy's assets. It was on the last page of the promissory note, in the little bitty small print, but the consequences of that tiny print were huge. It basically said that if something with the deal went sideways, then I could lose literally everything I own.

But in the world of private money there are no personal guarantees; not once, in the hundreds of deals I've done and the multiplied millions I've borrowed, have I ever had to sign a personal guarantee. My family's personal assets are safe and secure, regardless of what happens with any deal.

Now pause for a moment and take a look back over the information I've given you above. You can plainly see the advantages you'll enjoy by going the private money route.

Instead of expensive middlemen, unnecessary fees and costs, and lots of time and trouble, private money provides us a way to enjoy the biggest possible return from every investment.

With my **Where to Get the Money Now** system, you quickly and easily get the funds you need to make deals and reap big profits.

You can see that one huge advantage of dealing with private lenders is avoidance of entanglement with banks and institutions.

Private money also avoids the challenges of creating and maintaining a partnership with the lender.

Now let me explain, because this is very important: though I treat my private lenders like partners, <u>they are not partners</u>. I mentioned this before when I talked about interest rates.

The private lender does not own the property; you do. The private lender is not on the title; you are. You are the owner of the property. The private lender acts in exactly the same capacity as a bank; they will receive the same security as a bank. In North Carolina, where I live, it's called a Deed of Trust or mortgage.

Why is that important to you?

Let's compare business models: the old business model (equity partnership) and my revolutionary **Where to Get the Money Now** system.

Old business model: A lender puts up the money, and you do the work (searching for and finding the property, dealing with realtors and contractors, rehabbing and marketing the home, staging it for showings, etc.). The lender receives the mortgage, and the profits are then split 50/50 between the lender and you.

In my **Where to Get the Money Now** system:

You keep 100% of the profits!

Why do I want to give up half my profit when I'm already providing the lender an 8% return on their investment?

"But Jay, isn't the bank where all the money is?"

That's what most people think – if you want to fund deals, you have to go through some sort of official financial institution and play by their rules to get their limited amount of money. But do you have any idea how much private money is sitting on the shelf in the US right now, money that could be used to fund your deals?

Want to take a guess? Five hundred million dollars? A billion dollars? A trillion?

How about 18 trillion dollars? That's right – 18 TRILLION, sitting in money market accounts in cash, available to buy, rehab, and sell houses.

Now, when I was doing this with the banks' money, I had lines of credit. Those are limited, but private money is virtually unlimited.

And there's more coming all the time!!

Ten thousand baby boomers retire in this nation every day – the majority of those people have some sort of retirement money, right? What are they going to do with all that money?

Most of them are going to put it into an account that will return pennies on their investment versus what they'll be able to get through investing in real estate with you, when you use my **Where to Get the Money Now** system.

BIG REASON #3: CLOSE QUICKLY

Doesn't it surprise you that anything ever closes when banks are involved? Yet I'm able to buy many properties that my competitors would miss out on because I can close every deal with all cash in seven days. Seven days! (I've even been able to get a deal done in 24 hours.) With banks involved, you're looking at up to 45 days.

Time is a major factor in this business, so you don't want to waste it. Using private money, I get more offers accepted and more deals done because I can close so quickly. Recently I did a deal on a property for which the sellers were asking $60,000, but because I was able to close so quickly, I got the house for $57,500.

How can I close so quickly?

When I find a deal and have the funding, my assistant just completes a simple one-page, fill-in-the-blanks email that details the relevant information: the interest rate, the lender, the borrower, the property securing the loan, etc. The information is sent to my real estate attorney, who will have the paper work ready in 48 hours. The promissory note and deed of trust are ready for closing the next day.

Obviously, that kind of flexibility and efficiency is great for my bottom line, but as we've already seen, it's as good for everyone else involved as it is for you. Remember the dear lady being forced to sell her home for a fraction of its worth and move? Remember how I was able to offer to close fast, with all cash, and make it happen? That's a huge benefit both to you and to the seller, but I couldn't have made that offer by borrowing money from a bank.

So far, we've seen why this world of private money is the key to powering your dreams and fulfilling your personal and business vision – you can't lose with a system that allows YOU to…

- Make the rules
- Have all those advantages over having to deal with the banks
- Close quickly on deals you might otherwise have missed out on

Believe it or not, there's another BIG REASON why you need to be using private money to fund your deals RIGHT NOW! You're going to eat this up with a spoon! You ready to hear it? Well here it is because I've kept you waiting long enough…

CHAPTER 4

My Favorite Reason To Use Private Money

BIG REASON #4: Get Multiple Checks Every Deal!

This big reason is my number 1 favorite reason for using private money! And after I go through and tell you all about it, I'm sure it's going to be your number 1 favorite reason as well!

Let's just get right into it. My favorite reason to use private money is because I receive multiple checks on every deal.

Now I know most people get ONE big check when they sell a property. I do too. But you know what's great about this world of private money? That's only 1 check out of multiple checks that I get on every deal! So let's talk about the other checks!

Usually when you go to the closing table to buy a property, you've got to come up with 3, 5, 10, or 20 percent down depending on the deal. Well, I don't have to take any money to the closing when I purchase and invest in a property. AND I tell you what, when I was borrowing money from the banks and the mortgage companies for real estate investing, there was no such thing as receiving multiple checks.

You know in this wonderful world of private money, which again is just doing business with individuals and not banks, we don't bring any money to the closing table of our own, and we actually receive our first big check at the closing.

Let me put it another way... we get paid to buy a property! Now who here reading this right now wants to know how to get paid to buy a property?

When I tell people we're able to get big checks and close deals within a week, they're amazed. "How do you do it, Jay?" I'm asked a lot. I tell them the secret is relationships. Being able to develop great relationships is the key behind any successful business, especially when it comes to real estate investing.

In fact, recently, my wife, Carol Joy, and I walked into our real estate attorney's office and picked up a check for $49,739 after closing a deal. And check this out... just seven days before we met the seller of the house for the very first time, the negotiation began just seven days prior to closing!

This particular deal came to us through Facebook. We run two kinds of ads: one directed at buyers and one directed at motivated sellers. This seller responded to my Facebook ad; they wanted to do business with us because we offered to close the deal in seven days. We're able to fulfill that promise because this deal was funded by private money. We brought no money to the closing table and picked up a $49,739 check!

Wouldn't you love to pick up a check for almost $50,000 when you BUY a property? Now I'm sure the first question you're going to ask me is "Okay, how do I receive a check when I buy the property and bring no money to the closing table?"

It's very simple… we always borrow more money than required to buy the property.

Say wait a minute, who's going to loan me more money than I need to purchase the property, and how are they secure in doing that?

Obviously, we're doing this with individuals. Private lenders, individuals, are just like us. And the secret is relationships. Being able to develop great relationships is the key behind any successful business, especially when it comes to real estate investing.

Let me just use an example here. Let's take this hypothetical house that we're going to buy okay. Let's say you and I are in business together, and we're going to buy this house.

Now let's say this house has got an after repaired value of $200,000. When I say ARV, I mean knock em out, drop dead gorgeous, ready for a Southern Living magazine cover.

Let's first define what is an after repaired value, which by the way, in the business, we call our ARV. And you can determine the ARV through sold comps acquired from your realtor.

We may be buying this house, let just say… we're buying this house for $100,000 or 50% of the after repaired value. Now I'm going to have to write another book to tell you how I go about finding houses at 50% of the ARV, but for now, let me just let me just say I buy most of our properties at no more than 50% of the after repaired value.

Assuming you know how to find that deal, we're going to buy this after repair value of $200,000 house for $100,000.

Now, let's say the house needs rehab or repair. By the way folks, typically, you're not going to buy a house at 50% of the after repaired value unless it needs rehab.

Let's say the repairs on this house are $30,000. You can easily estimate repair costs, using my system, with a 15-minute walkthrough of the property. In fact, I teach this on my Live Event bus tours. If you'd like to join us for three inspiring days of training on North Carolina's gorgeous Crystal Coast, register now by going to https://www.JayConner.com/Conference.

In this world of private money, when we do business with a private lender, they not only are willing to give us 100 percent of purchase price, but they are also, in a lot of cases, willing to give us 100 percent of the rehab money, up front. That's because of our relationship with them.

Now a lot of people have a specific type of image in their head when they think of someone who "has money." They picture someone who always wears expensive clothes or lives a highfalutin lifestyle. The thing is that most people with money are smart. They don't advertise their money to everyone on the street. They've been wise and saved, or they have their money in an IRA. In fact, a good majority of the private lenders we do business with fall in that category.

As we tell our students at our live events, you can't judge somebody just by looking at them. Sam Walton drove a beat-up pickup truck even after he owned Wal-Mart for years. When asked why he drove the truck, he said, "What am I supposed to haul my dogs around in a Rolls Royce?" So don't judge anyone and just extend the offer to work with people and build long lasting relationships.

So back to that check that I'm walking away with at closing. That check is what we call the overage. By the way, let me tell you my favorite phrase that I see on my real estate attorney's check stubs when I pick up a check. In fact, earlier today, before I wrote this, we picked up a $32,000 check from buying a property, and it had my favorite phrase on it, "Excess cash to close."

I love excess cash to close!

I'm buying it for a hundred thousand. Rehab is say $30,000 in this example we're talking about. Now let's say, I mean you know, there's always marketing cost. There's carrying cost; there's utilities; there's etcetera etcetera until we get that house cash flowing or sold.

We might sell it on rent to own or least purchase. We might sell it on cash out or put it in the Multiple Listing Service or whatever. In that case, I'd say I want to borrow a $140,000 on that deal.

I borrow $140,000 from the private lender. The private lender wires their funds to the real estate attorney's trust account. I buy the house.

I got $40,000 left over because the purchase price was $100,000 right? $40,000 excess cash!

Now there's a little bit that would come out of that $40,000, and that would be my real estate attorney's fees. You know, title search, document preparation, etc. So I might bring home $39,500 on this deal.

In this example, when the after repaired value is $200,000, the most we would borrow is a $150,000 or 75% of the ARV from the private lender. And since we're only borrowing $140,000, we're below that 75% ARV, and I can bring home a check of $39,500 after attorney's fees.

So that's how you get paid to buy a house and get your first check! And you always want to borrow more than the purchase price, even if you're not going to rehab the property, because you have to consider things like marketing costs and carrying costs (utilities, insurance, taxes, etc.) associated with every property. So, you'll get your first big check after the closing documents are recorded on public record, just like a traditional closing.

We're straight on the first check right?

Okay, now let's talk about the second check.

If you, as the real estate investor, sell this house… if we, we've done this deal together, we're going to sell this house on rent to own, well, what are we going to collect?

We're going to collect a non-refundable option fee. Some real estate investors call it a lease option deposit. The legal term is actually an option fee.

And so the second check we receive we may get like a $10,000 or $15,000 option fee from the buyer of this house.

That's the second check. Let's hang out on that check for a second.

That check is our check. We received it. Now what's gonna happen in the future?

Well, that money is accounted for one of two ways.

First, if the rent to home buyer does not cash out, then that's a forfeited option fee that we now bring in as income, or we help them get ready for a mortgage… which we do… 80% of our rent to own buyers we cash out because we hold their hand in a credit repair program, and so now when they're ready for a mortgage, we apply that option fee to their closing cost or down payment or purchase price.

We're straight on the second check? An option fee from a rent to own buyer.

And then finally, the third big check is when we actually cash out on the house.

What I mean by cashing out on the house is either that rent to own buyer bought it and they got mortgage ready, or we put it in the Multiple Listing Service right up front, and we cash out. Now the check that we receive now in this wonderful world of private money is the difference between what we sell it for and what is still owed to the private lender.

In our example, I borrowed $140,000 from the private lender. We sell it for $200,000. That's the after repaired value. And of course, right now, the market I'm in is so hot, that as of this writing we're selling for full appraisal price, or if you sell on rent to own, you can actually price it for more than the appraisal price.

The check we're going to get is with the difference between what we sell it for ($200,000)... of course, if a realtor is helping to sell it, their fee is going to come out of it. And since we pay and accrue interest only payments to the private lender, we still owe the private lender $140,000.

We really get a $60,000 check, minus realtor and closing fees, in this example, when we sell the property, because we sell it for $200,000 and we still owe $140,000.

Now I got a real important point to make, but are we clear on the third check first?

Let's quickly review. You get the first check when you buy... difference between what you borrow and what you bought it for. The second check, if you sell it on rent-to-own. And the third check when you cash out.

But I want everybody to get this point big-time...

Obviously, we don't get to keep the $40,000 check and the $10,000 check and the $60,000, right?

That initial check you were getting, we're using for the rehab. We don't borrow that kind of money if there's not a rehab, you know.

However, in this wonderful world of private money, you can pull equity out at any time, for your business, if your business needs cash flow or whatever because you know the private lenders are so easy and flexible to work with.

So just to review real quick, you can get 3 BIG Checks when using private money.

1st When You Buy

2nd When You Sell Rent-To-Own

3rd When You Sell

Now, what I didn't mention is that if you sell on rent-to-own, you can also get multiple little checks every month… checks that we call cash flow! And that's the difference between what your monthly payments might be and what you're charging for rent.

Say for example on this $200,000 house, you borrowed $140,000 at 8% simple interest. That would be $933.33 per month, $2800 per quarter, or $11,200 per year. Hey, remember, you get to make the rules and decide when to make your interest payments.

If your monthly payments are say… $950 (I rounded for easy math), throw in taxes and insurance and say you owe $1250 per month, then if you rent out the house for $1750 per month, you've got a $500 per month cash flow check. And those keep coming month after month until that tenant buyer either buys the house from you or moves out!

Who now wants multiple checks for their deals?!?

Hey, I know this is all great stuff, and I'm sharing this with you, so that you can get on the fast track to raising millions of dollars in private money and avoid some of the mistakes I've made in the past. In fact, let me share with you the biggest real estate investment mistake I ever made!

MY BIGGEST REAL ESTATE INVESTMENT MISTAKE

In 2009, at the very height of the real estate boom, I bought three condos situated on the North Carolina coast. My intention was to rehab and flip them for a quick profit. Just one condo cost me $200,000 to purchase it; then I put $30,000 in it for rehab. By the time I got the three condos listed in MLS, the market had totally collapsed; I was totally unable to unload them.

Not only had the demand dried up, but so had the financing. The banks had quit lending, so I turned to private money and was able to raise $2,150,000 in 90 days. Without private money, I would have been finished in real estate.

But the point of the story is this: I got stuck with properties I had never intended to hold. Any good real estate investor knows this can happen; a lot of times, it's very hard to sell a property if you're relying only on MLS.

But I still had rental income from the condos, right? Yes, but... due to the seasonal nature of the demand, I still ended the year with a negative cash flow on the properties of $15,000. Ouch!

I was literally out of viable options when it came to these condos. If I were to sell the condos, I wouldn't even get back the initial cost. I rent them when I can, but the condos still cost me money every year. What's a real estate investor to do? The best way to avoid getting burned by a bad deal is to—guess what?—avoid a bad deal in the first place!

So where did I go wrong?

My mistake was in counting on being able to sell the condos and make money, but I hadn't done the calculations on whether I could afford to continue to own them if I was unable to sell them. So, here's the rule: <u>NEVER buy a property unless the rent you can receive from</u>

it will cover your expenses. When doing these calculations, be sure to take into account the following expenses:

- mortgage (principal and interest)
- insurance
- taxes
- HOA dues
- maintenance
- marketing costs
- vacancy rate

But if you decide to rent out the property at some point, does that mean you can't still decide to flip it later? Of course not! You can have any exit strategy you want, but ALWAYS run the numbers on the cash flow from the property if you're forced to hold it – and don't forget to count ALL your costs! Listen to and learn from the voice of experience!

When To Use Private Money

Great question! I'm glad you asked – any time a seller requires all cash, you'll use private money.

It doesn't matter if the property is listed in MLS, is a For Sale By Owner (FSBO), is bought at auction, or is being sold through any other kind of medium. When the seller requires all cash, use private money. But is there a time when you'll opt not to use private money? Yes, when using creative means of buying, like seller financing, buying subject to the existing note, buying on lease option, or getting an option to wholesale the property to another investor.

While we're on the topic of how we fund deals, let me address one question you may be asking yourself, "Is owner financing a realistic option in real estate investing?" The short answer, "no".

Look at it this way, if you talk to ten seller leads, how many do you think you could persuade to do owner financing? At most, one or two. But what do people want out of this transaction? They want cash.

The bottom line is this, without private money, I would have been out of this business a long time ago. Without private money, you will very likely drown in this business.

By the way, I have to share with you the magic question in your negotiations that I've learned over the years. This one question has saved me THOUSANDS of dollars on several deals! Are you dying to know what it is? Well, I'm dying to tell you. Of course before I do, I have to set the stage!

I taught this question to my acquisitionist many, many years ago, and let me tell you how well it works!

A few months ago, there's this house on Bridle Lane. In just six days, we went from having a motivated seller find my website to closing a deal that brought in over $60,000 in profit. During those six days, I spent only 1 1/2 hours of my own time working on the deal. Pretty good huh? This was all made possible because I have managed to automate my team and my processes.

But one detail that really stuck out to people was how we were able to bring the seller down from their initial asking price of $100,000 to the offer they took at $80,000. Making a successful offer on a house is key in this business – especially offers that benefit you and the seller.

When you or your acquisitionist asks what's the lowest price a seller will accept, the number you hear first is rarely the lowest number that will end up on the table. When my acquisitionist first got on the phone with the Bridle Lane seller, he insisted that the lowest amount he'd settle for was $100,000. Then, she asked the Magic Question.

You ready for it? You want to know what it is?

Well, here ya go, "If we could get you all cash, without needing to get approved for a mortgage, without ordering an appraisal, and close within seven days, what's the least you'll take?"

That one question saved me $20,000 instantly as the seller dropped his price to $80,000! That's a pretty good savings off the bat, but as always, you have to verify repairs before you make an offer.

Last year, I made a deal on another house not too far from Bridle Lane. The after repair value of the house was $175,000. The repairs were $80,000, and the seller wanted $80,000. The Magic Question got him down to $65,000. That was a $15,000 instant savings! One question, $15,000. Again, pretty good!

But after looking at the numbers, the best offer for us was $20,000. Yes, $60,000 below asking!

So, my acquisitionist offered $20,000 and justified the offer by explaining what needed to be done based upon what my contractor recommended. And guess what happened? Yes! The seller took the offer. He went from $80,000 asking to $65,000 to $20,000 cash, and he was happy about it! It was a win-win deal for both of us!

Hey, I developed this negotiation strategy over years of trial and error. I'll admit that I let great deals slip by early in my career because I didn't have a coach, and therefore, I didn't know how to make the right offer. Of course, I wouldn't be able to make these great offers today were it not for the private money I already have lined up before making offers.

But even if you can buy a property with all cash because you have the private money all lined up, there's one more way to finance deals that I want to share with you – a really cool strategy you're going to love, particularly if you're looking for a great buy-and-hold (it offers longer terms than a typical private money deal). As I mentioned, it's called "buying subject to," and it's a great option for you because it provides lower interest rates than private money and gives you one more source of funding for you deals.

When I say "subject to," I mean buying a home, or any property, *subject to* the existing mortgage. In short, I buy a house from a seller, the deed is transferred into my entity's name, and I agree to make the seller's mortgage payments. However, the mortgage stays in the seller's name until I sell the property to a new buyer.

Now, you might be asking, *"Who, in their right mind, would sell their house, leave the mortgage in their name, and trust you will make their payment?"*

This was the question I asked when I first heard about closing deals subject to the existing note. This method of buying properties sounded impossible!

There are plenty of reasons why I buy properties subject to the existing note, but who would be willing to sell me their house while still being responsible for the mortgage? For a seller, it sounds like a big risk. Where's the guarantee that I will pay their mortgage that remains in their name? When I first started talking to potential sellers about buying their properties "subject to," I quickly learned that the person that would take me up on that offer is a motivated seller.

It could be someone who desperately needs debt relief or who can't afford their mortgage payments, or it could be someone who doesn't want to go through the long process of an MLS listing because of an imminent move. Very often the properties I buy subject-to are already in foreclosure, and the payments are way past due.

Recently, I bought a house "subject to" from a seller who was four months behind on their payments. If the seller has a mortgage, I talk to them about selling subject to the existing note.

In order to buy a property "subject to," there has to be a current mortgage in place. Obviously, sellers who own their house free and clear of any mortgages aren't going to sell "subject to." On a free and clear house, I negotiate to buy with seller financing.

When I buy the house though, I'm providing a much-needed help to the seller by bringing their payments current and bringing the house out of foreclosure, thus improving their credit score. For me, buying subject to the existing note will always provide me with the most profitable deals. When you are buying "subject to," you will be paying the current mortgage's interest rate. So, if the interest rate on the existing mortgage is only 4%, that's a whole lot better than paying a private lender 8%. Once again, you can see how using my system results in wins all around.

It's also worth noting that houses you buy "subject to" are usually in good condition and need very few repairs. This is because the seller is usually still living in the home when you purchase it.

Not long ago, I went out with my acquisitionist to view a property. The sellers had painted, installed new hardwood floors, and updated the bathrooms. There was almost nothing that needed to be done. It was gorgeous!

The after-repair value on that house was $170,000. The seller had already agreed to sell it for what they owed, which was $118,000. "Oh, my lands!" Talk about a $52,000 profit with no rehab needed! But hey, let's say I did need some rehab. Maybe some new carpet and paint that might cost me $5,000. Can I use private money on this deal even if I'm buying it subject-to the existing mortgage?

Well, of course! With an after-repair value of $170,000, 75% ARV would be $127,500. That means I can borrow $9,500 from a private lender ($127,500 minus $118,000 equals $9,500). I can use $5,000 for repairs and use the remaining $4,500 for attorney fees, carrying costs, or whatever I want. Again, everyone wins!

Now that you see all the advantages of using private money in your real estate investment business, you're no doubt saying, "Where's this been all my life? I'm ready to put this to work right now!" But you may also be thinking, "It's obvious why I want to use private money, but why would a private lender want to do business with me?" Check this out...

CHAPTER 5

WHY DO PRIVATE LENDERS WANT TO DO BUSINESS WITH US?

So FAR WE'VE TALKED A lot about why we want to use private money – it's easy, fast, and flexible. It allows us to move quickly, so that we never have to miss out on a deal, and it gets us big (and little) checks on every property.

Now, let's turn things around for a moment – it's now obvious why we want to use private money, but why do private lenders want to have anything to do with us? Now why on God's green Earth would someone want to give us hundreds of thousands of dollars if not more? Well, let me tell you why…

BIG RETURNS

First, and most importantly, your private lender is going to earn a lot of money.

Do you have any idea what kind of interest Certificates of Deposit are getting these days? Go to http://www.BankRate.com and check it out. The last time I checked, the average was less than 1%! That's right! LESS THAN 1%. These are the kinds of piddly returns **potential** private lenders are getting on their money; they need you, and they just don't know it!

By the way, did you know that CDs actually have a negative return, when you factor in taxes?!? The banks are actually charging you to loan them your money!

So, what are private lenders supposed to do? They don't know!

Where on earth are they supposed to put their hard-earned money so that they get a great return?

They don't have any idea where to turn or what to do… and that's where we come in. You and I know exactly how and where they can get fantastic returns on their money and live the life they're dreaming about, too! It's our job—our moral and ethical obligation—to provide the answers to those questions and alleviate them of those problems.

Recently I had a private lender wire $120,000 to my real estate attorney for a deal – that money was in a savings account. It had been sitting in their bank over the previous 45 days, earning nothing.

Now that they've lent me that money to do a deal, they're going to earn 8% percent – that's an infinite amount of increase over what that money would have done for them!

Many people don't know that an individual can use his or her IRA, 401(k), or ROTH to lend as private money. I myself converted my own IRA into a self-directed IRA and became a private lender.

In fact, half of mine and Carol Joy's private lenders are investing their IRA retirement money with us. Until I told them, not one of them knew that they were able to lend money in this way and double or triple their returns.

Again, it's our obligation to educate the men and women in our warm market—our friends, family, and associates—about the huge blessing they can receive through the magic of private money.

A SAFE AND SECURE INVESTMENT

So, the first reason private lenders want to do business with us is the huge returns they're receiving on their money, but have you ever heard the principle that huge returns only come through huge risk?

When I do real estate deals with private money lenders, am I putting those lenders at high risk of losing their investment? Absolutely not!

When you educate your warm market about this opportunity, they'll want to invest with you because their investment is safe and secure! Let me explain...

The private lender's money is secure because he or she is getting the same security the bank gets: a mortgage, so in case of default, the lender gets the property. See, most people get that when they buy a house; they go to a bank and get a mortgage. And if after some time they stop making their mortgage payments, then the bank will go through this process called foreclosure. And after all is said and done, the bank gets the property as the collateral for their loan. In other words, the bank now owns the property... and that property is typically worth more than what they lent out, so that's how they protect themselves.

Right. What most people don't know is that as a private lender, they are now the bank! When they get the same paperwork that a bank would get, they get the same protections. If they lend you money to buy a house and you don't pay them, they can get the property from you as collateral. Plus, remember that conservative loan to value ratio (65-75%, as I showed you earlier)… that's further protection for their money!

All this means that the lender's investment isn't volatile – the principal loan amount doesn't go up and down in contrast to the stock market. They will always get their principle amount back in my program because I pay them interest only payments.

By the way, as a side note, one more advantage of private money investment in real estate over investment in stocks is when someone invests in stocks, they've already lost money through fees, commissions, etc. My private lenders get all of their principle back and don't pay any fees.

Consistent, Known Returns

As I just said, my private lenders do not incur any costs or pay any fees to loan me their funds. And when you follow my system, your private lenders won't either! You, the real estate investor, is responsible for all closing costs and associated fees. Because of that, the private lender always knows the exact Return on Investment (ROI) on every loan they make to you.

Another reason that your lenders will love this program is that the principal loan amount stays the same until the property sells. Therefore, your private lender is earning more money: by not paying any of the principle down, you are paying interest only. As a real estate investor, we love this part of the program because our payments are lower.

When I put together my **Where to Get the Money Now** system, I did everything I could to think of the perfect way to create wins for everyone involved: you, the seller, the buyer, and the private investor. Simply follow my system, and you'll see exactly what I'm talking about.

You quickly get unlimited funding for all your deals and huge returns on every transaction.

The seller gets fast relief from a bad situation, and a buyer gets a beautiful, like-new home.

And did you know that 70% of Americans cannot go to a bank and get a mortgage, so they can own their own home? Since I sell a lot of my homes by offering my rent-to-own program, I'm able to help buyers win and help them live the American dream of home ownership when they may not have been able to otherwise.

And a private lender gets returns they will not get anywhere else, without the concern of losing all their money. Forget win-win – how about win-win-win-win!

A lot of times, real estate investors get a bad rap. Some people believe we're just out to take advantage of others, but they don't understand what we do. But I'll tell you this – if a deal isn't a win for the seller, a win for the buyer, a win for the private lender, and a win for me, I'm not doing the deal!

I'm proud to be a real estate investor because I'm able to make a huge difference in the lives of others. I'm a problem solver – the seller has problems (debt, credit, etc.), the private lender has problems (money sitting around and not earning anything), and the buyer has problems (locating a beautiful, comfortable, yet affordable home).

With one deal, I can solve all those problems. That's what I do; that's what you're going to be doing – creating wins all around. But to create all those wins, we've got to get our hands on the money – how do we do that? I'm about to show you, and you're gonna love it…

CHAPTER 6

WHERE—AND HOW—TO GET THE MONEY

I DON'T KNOW ABOUT YOU, but I don't like to beg. And I know that some of you... as you've been reading about the magic of private money... may have been thinking, "All that sounds great, Jay, but I don't like to go around asking people for money." You know what? Neither do I.

That's why I don't do it – ever. And using my system, I don't have to! And when you use my **Where to Get the Money Now** System, neither do you!

I have yet to chase anyone or try to talk anyone into a deal. I've never had to beg.

I know, I know, you're thinking, "But Jay, how on earth do you get all that money if you never ask people for it?"

I'm so glad you asked!

As I mentioned to you in chapter two, your private money lenders are in one of two markets: your warm market (people you already know) and your cold market (existing private lenders).

Existing lenders already know how private lending works – they don't need to be educated about the amazing returns you're going to be providing them. You'll just get in touch with them, and you'll receive their funds. I'll teach you all about that later on, but for now, let's talk about your warm market...

YOUR WARM MARKET

Remember all those people we talked about in chapter two, with all that money sitting around in savings accounts and CDs, basically paying the banks for the use of their own money? They don't have any idea about the astronomical returns you can be giving them on their money, so it's our job to educate them! Not chase or beg them, you understand, but simply to educate them about what their money COULD be doing. When you turn them on to that, THEY will be chasing YOU. Sound awesome? It is!

When it comes to real estate investing and funding deals with private money, the big takeaway, and you'll always want to keep this foremost in your mind, is, "THE MONEY ALWAYS COMES FIRST!"

Now what I mean by that is that you always get the MONEY first before you get the deal! This is something I missed for many years and had to learn the hard way. So take it from me, so you don't make the same mistake – when funding deals with private money, the MONEY (not the deal) comes FIRST!

Check out the following scenario featuring "Glenn," a fictional potential private lender.

Let's say that Glenn is in my warm market – he's someone I have a relationship with through church, Rotary, family, etc. I'm having a casual conversation with Glenn about my private money program, or using my PowerPoint presentation, and I tell him about a deal I've got and that I'd like him to fund it.

Now what have I just done? I've compromised my position! Why?

First of all, I've come across as desperate – what Glenn hears is, "I've got a deal under contract, and I need you to fund it, or I'm in trouble."

Secondly, I've asked Glenn to make too many decisions in too short a time, "does he like the program, does he want to fund the deal, can he help me out before I run out of time in the next 30 days, etc." I've entirely compromised my position and, in all likelihood, have just talked my way out of a deal.

Instead of approaching Glenn that way, here's what I'll do... I'll only talk to him about the money. No discussion of a deal, just the money; what my program offers HIM and how it's the answer to HIS needs. Of course, he's going to love it, and at that point, I get from Glenn a verbal pledge; now, he's on board.

Then, a few days later, when I've got a deal, I go back to Glenn, and I keep it simple. I tell him only the four things he wants to know:

1. What city or area of town the property is located?
2. The After Repaired Value of the property.
3. The money required to do the deal.
4. The closing date on the property.

Notice I did not tell Glenn the street and street number; I didn't tell him the purchase price of the home – why not? Because I'm trying to hide something from him? No, because he just doesn't care!

Notice also that I told Glenn the money required to do the deal. I did not ask him if he wanted to do the deal. He's already told me he's interested!

The reason I tell Glenn the closing date is because that's the deadline by which the money must be wired to the attorney. (If we haven't done business before, I'll need to email very specific wiring instructions to him.)

Now, what's the big takeaway from all this? You already know, "the MONEY always comes FIRST!"

Now that we've got that essential concept down, let's talk about the five steps to getting the money from your warm market.

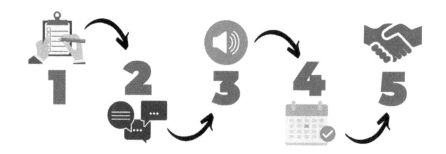

Step 1: Identify Your Top Potential Private Lenders

Go through your email list, your cell phone contact list, your Christmas card list, your Facebook friends, every list of people and contacts you have.

When you come to my Private Money Academy Conference, I'm also going to share with you my very own Magic 44 system: forty-four categories of people you know. You may not realize it, but there are millions and millions of dollars in your contact lists – we just need to figure out where it is. When we do, we have our list of top potential private lenders.

STEP 2: HAVE A CONVERSATION

You can do this over the phone or in person; it doesn't matter, but you're just going to have a simple, casual conversation with each potential lender on your list.

After some pleasantries and a bit of chitchat, the conversation may go something like this:

You:

"Emily, as you probably know, I'm investing in real estate these days. I'm taking advantage of the tidal wave of foreclosures going on right now, and I've got something to tell you that very, very few people know about. In fact, the only way people know anything about it is if I tell them. What I'm about to tell you is by referral only and by invitation only. You see, Emily, I've now opened up my real estate investing business to people I know and trust…"

Now, what did you communicate to Emily when you told her you were opening up your business to people you know and trust? That you didn't have to include her in this great opportunity, but you did because of the relationship of trust you have. What you didn't communicate to Emily was, "I'm broke and desperate, so I've got to beg everyone I can think of for money."

You:

"I have a program that may or may not be for you."

What did you communicate to Emily when you said that the program may or may not be for her? I completely took the pressure off her; she knows right away that you're not going to try to talk her into anything.

You:

"Emily, I'm paying up to twenty times as much in returns as most folks can get through traditional investments. But unless you answer 'yes' to the following question, there's no need for me to send you any information. The question, Emily, is this, 'Do you have investment capital or retirement funds that aren't giving you a high rate of return safely and securely?'"

That's (literally) the million-dollar question!!

"Do you have investment capital or retirement funds that aren't giving you a high rate of return safely and securely?" I ask that question, every time, in those exact words. Do you think I have it memorized? Do you think it's worth memorizing for your own warm market conversations as well?

"Do you have investment capital or retirement funds that aren't giving you a high rate of return safely and securely?" I ask the question – then I do something that's very hard for me to do.

I shut up. I don't say anything. I wait for a response.

What if the answer is "no"?

Then he or she is broke! There's no reason to continue digging a dry well.

But if the answer is "yes, I do have investment capital or retirement funds," we move on to…

STEP 3: GIVE THEM MY STRESS-FREE INVESTING CD

The next thing to do is tell the potential lender that you would like to share with them a 16-minute recording called "Stress-Free Investing" on CD or MP3. By the way, I'll record your CD for you, and you can get my word-for-word script all inside my **Where to Get the Money Now** course. Simply take the script and record it yourself on your computer or at a local recording studio. You can also convert it to a YouTube link.

Now, the purpose of the recording is not to sell the potential lender on your private money lending program; it's only 16 minutes. It doesn't go into detail about your program. It just introduces and explains private lending and gets the potential lender's greed glands all swelled up in their neck. You want to arouse their curiosity and make them want to hear the details.

The recording itself won't reveal your interest rate and doesn't disclose the geographical area you're working in. It won't tell them how they'll get their money back if you lose your mind and run off to the Caribbean (yes, we have that covered). To get them really interested, we raise all these questions at the end of the recording, but it's in step four that we spill the beans.

And oh! This recording is something you need to have with you at all times. Either put a bunch of CDs in your car, so you have them handy, or put it in a format you can email or send directly from your phone.

But whatever format you decide on, it is essential that you be ready at all times to get this recording into your warm market. After all, there's a lot of truth to the saying that "success is when opportunity and preparedness meet and shake hands." Let me show you what I mean...

I met Floyd, a man whom I'd never met before in my life, at a community event a few years ago. As we shook hands, I noticed that he smelled like money, so I offered him my 16-minute recording. Other than assuring him it had nothing to do with Multi-Level Marketing, I said very little about what the CD actually says. I just let the recording do its job. Seven days later Floyd became my newest $500,000 private lender. It was really that simple!

Trying to sell someone on the CD before they're even introduced to the idea of private lending is the kiss of death! Just let the recording do its job.

Talking it up before they've listened to it is totally counterproductive. Instead, play on the insatiable curiosity we all have and make them want to hear more from you. When you have the right tools and use them correctly, less really can be more!

Step 4: Follow Up With A One-On-One Appointment

I'm going to get right down to street level and give you all the information you need to conduct this meeting in the next chapter, but for now let me hit a couple of highlights:

The beauty of my system is that this can take place in person or via telephone, conference call, or webinar. There is no limit to your potential to raise private money. I borrow private money all across the nation, and currently I have private lenders in seven states.

When conducting your meetings, just use my PowerPoint presentation. It's available for everyone who owns my **Where to Get the Money Now** system. When you get my system, you can go to the Students Only area at jay.conner.com and get it for yourself. The presentation is generic so that you can fill in your own interest rate, terms, etc. And if you'd like some free stuff, just email me at info@jayconner.com and ask for (and I'll give you) a list of current resources we use for conference calls and webinars. This will allow you to do the presentation anywhere!

Keep in mind though, for any potential private lenders who are local, always do a face-to-face meeting. They're a lot more personable, but webinars are great for meeting with folks who are out of your area.

Plus, it's important to make maximum use of your time – it takes the same amount of time to go over the program with eight people on a webinar as it does for just one. The only difference is that you can't ask for a verbal pledge, but through the use of my PowerPoint presentation via webinar, you'll get bigger results in the same amount of time.

Step 5: Ask For And Receive The Verbal Commitment

Hey, remember that one of the great things about my **Where to Get the Money Now** system is that I do everything I can to protect the

Private Lender's money. So I never ask them to send me money directly or put it in my own personal account or have it unsecured or anything. I only get a verbal commitment from them, so that I know how much they can invest and by when. This way, it gives me time to find a deal for them and/or work with them to transfer their funds into a Self-Directed IRA (which I'll tell you about later) or whatever we need to do in order to get their funds ready to go. Then, when I have a deal ready for them, I'll call them up and have them wire their funds to my attorney's escrow account.

Again, I do NOT tell them to send me the money. If they send it directly to me, that opens up a whole can of worms that I don't want to deal with, and it's not professional. Having a system, like my **Where to Get the Money Now** System, shows people that you're a PROFESSIONAL Real Estate Investor that knows what their doing, giving them the confidence to work with you!

BONUS STEP: CASH THE CHECKS AND HAVE SOME FUN!

Of course, you have to use the checks to actually buy, fix, and flip the property, and when you do, you get a big old check for your Hip National Bank and can re-invest some of it and spend some of it! I mean, why do this business if you're not going to enjoy some of it! And hey, this isn't a book on financial management and of course, with every big check, give back 10%, pay yourself 10%, pay your bills, and invest the rest! Enjoy the fruits of your labor!

So, there's your step-by-step guide to unlocking your warm market private money vault. I've got a lot more detail about this process later in the book, but that will do for now. Later on, I'll also give you everything you need to know to unlock big money through the private lender luncheon, so keep on reading!

Your Cold Market

O.k., I get it. Some of you are thinking, "But Jay, all my friends are broke and have no money!" I know, it's like I'm reading your mind right? And instead of talking to your broke friends or family, you want to talk to EXISTING private lenders, people you don't know who are already lending money on properties, right? Sounds pretty good doesn't it? It'd be just like fishing in a barrel!

Well, I call this my cold market strategy! How to raise millions of dollars from existing private lenders – people with money, sitting on it, ready for you to bring them your program and net them some big returns.

But where do you find these lenders? Do you want to know? Do you want to learn my system, so you can talk to these people? Of course you do!! So let me spill the beans...

You'll find all these people in my private lender data feed! As one of my students, I'll provide you with access to over 12,000 lenders who are just what you're looking for. All this information comes from public records, so we're not talking about any hard money or commercial money. It's all from private lenders. And every month, I have a software that goes out and finds all these people and serves them up on a silver platter for you!

Now, here's the secret sauce when it comes to dealing with existing private lenders: unlike the warm market, I'm not going to offer my program. I don't have to educate them about how all this works – they're existing private lenders. They already know the game and how it works, so instead of telling them what returns I offer, I ask them what they are accustomed to getting. I find out how they're used to dealing with real estate investors. When they say they're used to getting a 5% return, I'm not going to argue with them. Even if I normally pay my private lenders 8%, if you tell me you're happy with 5%, well I'm happy too!

While we're on that subject, please take special note of this… do not borrow unsecured money. This means do not take money unless it's collateralized or secured by a property. Doing so puts you in a position you don't want to be in – your private lenders aren't protected. A private lender will say to you—and I've had this happen many times—"What do I do? I'm ready to write you a check!" No, no, NO! No funds ever come directly to us – we don't receive our money until after the deal is closed and the documents recorded! Doing this protects them AND you! Plus, it shows them that you're a professional! There's no funny stuff going on here! You're on the up and up and doing things the right way! Everyone wins!

Once I've identified a potential lender from my private lender data feed, I'm going to use two letters. These are included in my **Where to Get the Money Now** system and are available in the manual, as well as in the Students Only area at www.jayconner.com. These two letters are the Fellow Investor letter and the Hot Buyer's List letter. These are not open solicitation letters. (I'll tell you what open solicitation is and why you want to avoid it in just a moment.) In the private lender data feed, you can do mail merge, task manager, and mail out.

The purpose of these letters is to establish a relationship with the lender. I simply tell them that I'm a real estate investor, that I found them in public records, and that through those records it looks like they're interested in real estate investing. When they respond to your letter, you can talk about doing business together. That will lead to a one-on-one appointment, from which you'll receive the lender's verbal pledge.

Whether your private lender comes out of your warm market or your cold market, what documents will he or she receive? A promissory note and a mortgage. Never enter into a merely verbal agreement on any deal, regardless of the nature of the relationship between you and the private lender.

Your private lender will be named as the mortgagee on the insurance policy and as an additional insured on the title policy. Inform your lender as to when they can expect the recorded mortgage and the promissory note. They don't have to see them up front before closing, but you will want to keep them informed as to when they can expect to have them. I've provided you with an example of the note, as well as some other documents, in the back of this book.

"Jay, should I provide the private lender with an appraisal of the property?"

That's the question I get all the time from my students. And guess what? I've never been asked for an appraisal or for a comparable market analysis (CMA) from anyone in my warm market. I simply tell them what the property's value is.

In the cold market, however, the lender might want to see the CMA, which you'll obtain from your realtor. If the lender asks for an appraisal—and this is very important—always provide an After Repaired Value appraisal. Most of the time, though, you won't have to provide either an appraisal or a CMA.

Before we go any further, let me address finding private lenders through open solicitation. "Open solicitation" refers to advertising your program and seeking investors through media, such as TV or radio spots, newspaper ads, direct mail, etc. Sounds great, right? But here's the catch... and this is also the reason I don't openly solicit... when soliciting from people you don't know, you can only borrow from an accredited investor.

At the time of this writing, an accredited investor is someone who has earned $200,000 individually or $300,000 jointly in the last two years or has a net worth of at least one million dollars. Now why would I want to put myself in that box? Why would I want to restrict my access to unlimited private money by openly soliciting? I wouldn't!

You see, when you're getting money from your warm market, the open solicitation limitation doesn't apply because these are people you already know. That means you can ask Uncle Joe or Aunt Sally or even little Tommy down the street whose grandmother has been giving him a $10,000 gift every year for the past 10 years into a savings account. They don't need to be making $200,000 a year for the past 2 years or even have $1,000,000 net worth. If they got money and want to lend it to you, great!

But what about the cold market, you may ask – why doesn't the open solicitation restriction apply there? Great question! The reason is that through the use of my letters, as described above, you've established a relationship with the lender.

An added benefit is that with my **Where to Get the Money Now** System, you're staying in compliance with the Federal Communications Commission and the Securities Exchange Commission. By avoiding all that bureaucratic red tape, I've got students who are getting hundreds of thousands of dollars in less than thirty days! You can too, by using the same system I personally use every single day to attract millions in private money. It's all part of my **Where to Get the Money Now** System.

PROVEN STRATEGIES FOR GETTING THE WORD OUT

In the preceding scenario, I showed you an easy, step-by-step process by which you can access millions in private money from your warm and cold markets. But before we leave this discussion, I want to put some more tools in your private money toolbox. Here are six more powerful, proven strategies for getting the word out about what you have to offer potential private lenders.

1. ATTRACT MILLIONS WITH ONE SENTENCE

Some time ago, my wife, Carol Joy, helped her mother celebrate her 80th birthday. The family put on a big birthday party, and partway through the afternoon, I found myself sitting at a large, round table, eating a slice of cake. Across from me sat a woman I recognized as someone who went to church with Carol Joy's mother. I hadn't seen her for years, so we got to talking. She asked me, "Jay, what are you doing these days?"

This is an ordinary question, but I cannot begin to tell you how pleased I was that she asked. Most people might answer this question by saying something like, "Oh, I'm a real estate investor." But not me! In fact, answering this question the right way is part of how I have received millions in funding from private money. It's part of a strategy I've developed, and anyone can answer this question and utilize a strategy that has nothing to do with your credit, income, or experience.

So anyway, whenever someone asked me what I do for a living, I give them this answer, *"I teach private lenders how to get higher rates of returns on their investment capital or retirement accounts than they can probably get anywhere else."*

This one question has raised me MILLIONS of dollars! It's funny though because more often than not, I'm met with a deer-in-the-headlights stare because they're trying to figure out what I mean by "private lenders."

At this point, I put on my teacher's hat because most people are very interested to learn how I'm able to get someone higher rates of returns on their investment capital or retirement accounts. Think about it. With this one sentence, I've piqued their curiosity about what I do and let them know I could possibly benefit them. This opens the door for me to tell them more about private lending and how they can perhaps become a private lender themselves.

So, at the birthday party, when this woman asked me what I did for a living, I told her, "Funny you should ask. Since I last saw you, I have started to teach private lenders how to get higher rates of returns on their investment capital or retirement accounts than they can probably get anywhere else."

As expected, I got a period of dead silence before she asked, "Now, what did you just say?" We kept talking, and I told her all about private lending. Soon, I learned her husband had a $700,000 IRA, and he wasn't happy with the returns he was getting.

The very next day, this woman invited me to her house, where I visited with her husband and had an amazing conversation about private lending. You can probably guess what happened next after this couple opened the door to being my next private lenders.

This is one of many strategies I've developed to successfully attract all the funding I need to never miss a deal. Anyone in real estate investing has missed out on a deal at some point in time, and you know how rough it is when the cause is lack of funding. That's why I regularly share these strategies here, as well as on my online video blog.

If you're interested in learning more strategies, then come on out to my next Private Money Academy Conference where I spill all the beans! Remember, as a bonus for purchasing this book, I've given you two tickets to attend at a value of $2,995 each! Get yourself registered now at https://www.JayConner.com/Conference.

By the way, it's a very natural progression to hand someone your 16-minute CD after making this curious introduction. Your 16-minute CD is your business card. After making your introduction, say, "Here's a CD I made that you may find interesting." I don't typically follow up with these contacts; they have my info on the CD, so they can reach out to me if they're interested and have funds to lend.

2. Two-on-Ones

What on earth is a "two-on-one"? When just starting out in your real estate business, you may not have the credentials or experience to start getting private money in meetings with potential lenders. The "two" in the "two-on-one" is you plus an experience real estate investor; the "one" is the potential private lender.

When you bring along a buddy who's done successful deals before, you automatically give yourself credibility. To prepare for these meetings, consider creating an LLC with your real estate investor friend and do some deals as a joint venture. Where do you find such seasoned real estate investors? Meetups for real estate investing clubs are perfect. When you attend and pitch why others should work with you, tell them that you can bring in private money and they can bring the experience.

3. Groups

Get the word out to clubs, associations, your church, and other organizations. In groups to which you're already a member, you can confidently share that you'll be putting on an educational seminar, for example. Present a 45-minute session that will teach them how they can get a higher return on their money than they can likely get anywhere else. For groups in which you aren't a member, join them with the intention of sharing what you do.

4. Business Networking International (BNI)

BNI is a networking group with chapters in your area. I recommend that you visit and join one or two BNI groups. This is a unique organization; everyone else in the group essentially functions as salespeople who can spread the word about what you do (as long as you're willing to do the same for them!).

5. SCORE

This is a nonprofit that helps small business owners grow their businesses. Most of the volunteers working at SCORE are retired executives. Do you see the potential in that? Approach SCORE with your private lender presentation and ask them to critique it. The benefits are twofold: first, they'll probably give you some valuable suggestions on how to make your presentation better. Second, the odds are pretty high that at least one or two of these retired executives will be receptive to your pitch!

6. REFERRALS

A study of folks thinking about buying a new car yielded great insight into human behavior – insight you can learn from and use in your real estate business. Here's what the study found: let's say that you're in a room with 100 people in the market for a new car. Sixty-seven of those people already know where they're buying their next car: at the last place they bought, because of a positive experience. Thirteen people in the room will respond to some form of advertising. But twenty of those looking for their next car are going to turn to their friends for a recommendation about where to shop. They aren't satisfied with their current dealership, but they don't have any idea where they should go. They aren't going to respond to direct mail or other advertising. They're going to talk to their friends.

What do these car shoppers have to do with us real estate investors? The numbers apply to our business as well. About 20 percent of folks with investment capital aren't happy with their current results.

They're considering doing something else with their funds, but they aren't sure what to do, so guess where they'll turn? That's right: to their friends, to find out what kinds of returns they're getting. Now, twenty percent of the investment capital available in the US may not sound like much, but as we learned above, it totals about $18 TRILLION! What can you do to get your share of that $18 trillion? One of your most effective methods will be referrals.

So how should you begin? As a real estate investor seeking private money, you're looking to do business with private lenders who have the most money to lend, right? Typically, the higher up the financial totem pole a person is, the less likely they are to use and respond to traditional advertising, like yellow page listings or direct mail. It's even unlikely they'll take the time to do an Internet search such as, "Where can I get a high rate of return on my investment?"

No, private lenders have a very different mindset when it comes to seeking services they want or need.

Think about it: if Warren Buffett is suffering from back pain, how likely is it that he'll look for a chiropractor in the yellow pages? He's not going to respond to a direct mail ad for back pain relief. Instead, he's going to call up one of his fellow billionaires—Bill Gates, maybe—and say, "Hey, Bill! I've got some back pain and need to see a chiropractor; who do you use?" It's just as simple as that; people who are financially well-off turn to one another for referrals.

The same principle applies to wealthy individuals, who have investment capital or retirement funds and want to get high rates of return. They aren't going to look up an investment firm online or through any other traditional channel. After all, "birds of a feather flock together," right?

They're going to ask their friends, "What kinds of return are you getting on your investment capital?" If they like the answer, they'll follow up with, "Where are on earth are you getting those great returns?" When they receive the answer, what do you think they'll do? That's right – they'll put their money in the same place.

HOW TO GET REFERRALS—ON PURPOSE

Let me finish this chapter by teaching you how to get referrals on purpose. You see, most business owners get referrals by accident. They're not actively, intentionally seeking referrals, but they did something right for a client, and that client then happens to mention their positive experience with the business to a friend. But that's too uncertain for the real estate investor who desires to really see his or her business take off.

Many of the referrals I've received have come from my current private lenders. Network through your current private lenders; ask if they know others looking to invest, who are interested in high rates of return.

More specifically, talk to all of your local lenders. Take them to lunch; show honest and sincere appreciation. Tell them you're trying to grow your business and ask them if they know anyone who may be interested in working with you.

Most importantly, talk them through all the potential referrals they could give you: family, friends, co-workers, church members, etc. When a private lender gives you a contact who turns into a new private lender, send a handwritten note of thanks to the lender who gave you the reference.

Another, and very effective, means of getting referrals is to make your private lenders say, "Wow!"

When your current private lenders are saying, "Wow!', you can be sure they're going to be so excited and happy with their experience with you; they're going to be telling their friends and family about you.

But how do you create the "Wow!" factor to get these referrals that are so vital to your business? How can you be sure that you're the person they're talking about when they talk about receiving high rates of return? You want satisfied private lenders making referring their friends to you, don't you? But how?

Folks don't usually talk about their experience with a business unless it was a bad experience. As a real estate investor, you want to go above and beyond in order to break this tendency. You want to make your private lenders so happy, they talk to their friends about you. You want to create "bragging rights experiences."

These are the kinds of experiences that turn private lenders into storytellers – and their stories are all about you and the fantastic service you've provided and the high rates of return you've given them! In other words, you've made your private lenders say, "Wow!'

So how do you "Wow!" your private lenders? Well, let me tell you how!

Treat them just as you would want to be treated. For instance, always pay your lenders on time (or even early!). Keep your word in every situation. Nothing destroys trust more than not doing what you say, when you say you'll do it. And in this business, lack of trust will put you out of business.

Another important way you can "Wow!" your private lenders is by showing honest and sincere appreciation. Write your lenders a handwritten note on the date they became your lender. A simple "Happy Anniversary!" note, thanking them for making a difference in your business, truly goes a long way.

When you are diligently and faithfully working your program, and you're not only going to give your private lenders higher rates of return than they're going to get using traditional means, that's a great big "Wow!" right there! But when you treat your private lenders as I've outline above, they can't help but say "Wow!" at the thoughtful and personal service you've given them. And I promise you – when you give them that kind of experience, they WILL tell their friends about it, and your phone WILL soon be ringing.

CHAPTER 7

THE ONE-ON-ONE APPOINTMENT

THE PREVIOUS CHAPTER DETAILED THE steps you'll follow to establish a private lender relationship, whether in your warm market or your cold market. In this chapter, I want to hang out for a while on the details of the one-on-one meeting. This is your meeting with the potential warm market private lender. Of course, every step of my 5-Step process is important, and one has a lot of details to cover, so I want to make sure you completely understand everything, so it goes as smoothly as possible.

The most important thing to understand here is that these items are non-negotiable. Remember, you set the rules! This is THE program. We're not telling folks "I pay folks between 6%-10%" and haggling with them over rates or terms." This is YOUR program, run by YOUR rules. You tell the private lender how your program is set up, and they agree to get onboard or they don't, but you're not in a negotiation.

Got it?

Let me give you an example. Remember me meeting Floyd a few pages back? After we'd done a couple of deals, Floyd said, "Jay, I don't want to do the private lending thing anymore. I want to joint venture with you and split the profits."

I replied, "It's been a pleasure doing business with you, Floyd, but I don't do that." No and's, but's, or if's. Or as the saying goes, "Too many cooks in the kitchen burn the grits!" You don't have to be nasty about it, but you do have to be firm in your own mind and in your communication with others – do not negotiate.

That may be a little scary to you – you might feel like you need to change things up a little here or there to keep the money flowing. Trust me – you don't. Remember how much private money's out there? It started with a "T," right? It's virtually unlimited, correct? So don't stress over it – there's always more private money. By the way, Floyd himself ended up giving me more money!

Your Private Money Program

So, you've scheduled your one-on-one appointment with a potential private lender, and now you're sitting down with him or her or them. If you have my **Where to Get the Money Now** System, I've put everything together for you already in a nice, slick PowerPoint Presentation. All you have to do is modify it for your business and off you go! If you don't have my system yet, I recommend you get it, so you don't have to recreate all this, and of course, I understand if for some reason you're unable to get it at this time and you need to spend the time and go about creating your own and see if it works. If that's the case, then here are some of the things you should definitely include in your program.

WHO ARE YOU?

First, you want to discuss who you are and why are you in this business. Share your vision and mission with everyone. People appreciate people working towards something more than just making money. While there's nothing wrong with making a lot of money, people want to know the reason behind it. This will help set the tone of the presentation and open everyone up to your purpose.

WHAT IS PRIVATE MONEY?

Next, of course, people want to know what exactly private lending is, so tell them. I covered this for you in Chapter 2 of this book, so you can just take some of what I wrote and repurpose it for your needs.

WHY BE A PRIVATE LENDER?

Along with that, you should tell them why they want to work with you and become a private lender themselves. I wrote about this already as well in Chapter 5 of this book. Boy, I'm making this real easy for you, aren't I?

HOW THINGS WORK

Next, you want to give them an overview of how everything works. Talk about finding the deal, the closing process, the paperwork they're going to get, etc. Remember, all closings are handled by a real estate attorney.

In some states, closings are sometimes handled by escrow companies and title companies, as well as real estate attorneys, but in the world of private money, we stick with real estate attorneys for closings. I've got some sample paperwork at the end of this book. Take my sample promissory note template to your real estate attorney and have him or her use them as templates when you do your first deal.

And don't forget to tell them about the insurance. Always protect your private lenders by naming them as the mortgagee in the insurance policy. In case of a loss (from fire, hail, etc.), private lenders get paid first.

And while I'm talking about protecting your private lender, make sure you tell them about the maximum total loan to value. As we've already discussed, it's 75% (but if the purchase price is $100,000 or less, the maximum loan to value is 65%). Here's why: 75% of $200,000 is a $50,000 equity cushion for the private lender, right? But 75% of $100,000 is only an equity cushion of $25,000.

TERMS OF ENDEARMENT

Ok. Let's move on. Next, tell them all about the payment details. This includes the following:

1. Length of Note.
2. Interest rates.
3. Interest-only payments.
4. Simple interest.
5. No penalty assessed for early payoff.
6. The minimum investment.
7. No private lender fees.

I already covered most, if not all of these in the book already, but here's a quick review of what I do in my program... remember, you set the rules for your program, so you may choose to make it slightly different.

1. Length of Note – A two-year term for investment capital; A five-year term for retirement money.
2. Interest rates – I pay 8% for first position (that is, the money I'm using to purchase the house) and 10% on junior positions.
3. Interest-only payments – This helps you with cash flow while preserving their principle amount.
4. Simple interest – I don't use compound interest. It keeps things simple.

5. No penalty assessed for early payoff – This means there's no prepay penalty for me. Of course, I usually just move the private lender's money to another property, so I don't pay off early very often.

6. The minimum investment – My minimum is $25,000. Of course, you may need less.

7. No private lender fees – There are none. I pay everything. The private lender pays nothing.

SHOW ME THE MONEY

Pretty straight forward right? So next, discuss how the private lender is going to get paid. I'll just list some points and discuss it all at once here.

1. Frequency of payments – I typically pay once or twice a year. Again, it keeps things simple.

2. 90-day call option – I offer all my private lenders what I call the 90-day call option. It's written right into the promissory note. All they have to do is give me 90 days notice, and I'll cash them out, with no penalty to the private lender. But remember – this is YOUR program. If the 90-day option scares you to death, don't offer it. If you want to charge a penalty for early withdrawal, write it into the promissory note. I don't charge a penalty if they call the note early, but you can if you like.

3. Disbursement of funds – The private lender never gives you any money – all funds are wired to your real estate attorney.

Before I move onto the next item, let me take a moment and discuss how important it is that you get funds WIRED to your attorney instead of getting checks. Some time back I had a private lender overnight a cashier's check to me, payable to my real estate attorney's trust account. Do you know how long it took that overnight package to get to me? A whole year! The package had a tracking number on it, of course, but one post office is saying it's in Abilene, Texas, and another is saying it's in Morehead City, North Carolina.

Now, this didn't bother me because I've got all the private money I need, but it bothered my private lender very badly. He's got a significant amount of money in no-man's land; it's not making him any money, and you can't stop payment on a bank check for ninety days. So guess what? No more overnighted checks!

Have your private lender send the funds by wire – no exceptions. I'm happy to pay the private lender's wiring fee of $30 for some peace of mind for everyone involved. The only private lenders I allow to use bank checks and cashier's checks are those who are local and who are going to deliver the check in person to the closing agent.

One more item related to security in the wiring of funds – always be in charge of giving out the wiring instructions. I had a closing recently in which my private lenders were scammed into wiring their funds to another country. The lenders got their money back because it was a bank error, but these are the kinds of things we want to avoid. It's easy to do so be taking a few common-sense steps. Again, always be the one giving out the wiring instructions.

WHERE TO FIND THE MONEY NOW

Ok., so what's next? Well, that's about it. I usually talk a bit about different sources of funding that they can use. They already know about certificates of deposit, money market accounts, savings accounts, and investment capital. But they may not be aware that they can use their retirement account to loan that money out to you and receive big returns, penalty- and tax-free!

Self-Directed IRAs

If you don't already have a retirement account with a self-directed IRA provider, I strongly suggest you open one, even if you don't do anything with it. You can open this account for a small deposit. Here's why you want to do so, you're going to be educating your potential private lenders on transferring their retirement funds into a self-directed IRA. You gain credibility with them when you say, "I have one of these accounts myself."

Not only do you want to open a self-directed IRA, but it's very important that you establish a relationship with a representative of a self-directed IRA company. I can then offer to set up a three-way phone call between my potential private lender, my IRA company representative, and myself, or I can just say to the potential private lender, "Do you want me to set up a conversation with the representative?"

If that works for the private lender, just give his or her cell phone number to the IRA representative and have your rep text them and set up a meeting. Then, all the private lender has to do is sign one document with the IRA company, and that company will handle everything else.

Many private lenders are reluctant to contact their retirement account administrator, and this way they don't have to. The IRA company rep contacts the company holding the private lender's funds and takes care of the transfer, and the self-directed IRA is typically funded in two to four weeks. This relationship between you and the self-directed IRA company rep is a crucial component to keeping your business running smoothly.

If there is any question about whether the private lender is able to move funds from their retirement account, simply have them contact their fund administrator and ask.

Home Equity Line of Credit (HELOC)

Another source of private money is a home equity line. If your private lender has equity in any property, they can act like a bank. They can borrow money on the equity at a small rate and loan it out to you at 8-10%. They're not loaning out their own money. They're loaning out the bank's money, and they pocket the spread.

I was talking to a potential private lender not long ago and mentioned the equity loan. He said, "What about land? I've got a farm here in North Carolina that's free and clear."

I suggested he contact his banker and get a line of credit collateralized by the farm. When we started talking, the private lender had $20,000. By leveraging his farm, he ended up with a lot more. Pretty cool, huh?

Portfolio Loans

And one more option is a portfolio loan. If a private lender has investment capital at a stock brokerage, the lender is already approved to borrow up to 50% of the current face value of the account. It takes about two weeks to get the portfolio loan account established. With this method, they can stay invested with their brokerage or stock portfolio and make even more (and more secure) money by investing with you.

So that's about it. Remember to keep it as simple and easy as possible. A confused mind does nothing, so you don't want to confuse your prospects. Give them enough to explain everything and then calmly and patiently answer any questions they may have. If you give them too much, they'll be overwhelmed and confused and won't do anything. Sometimes a confused mind is a scared mind, and you don't want to scare them from working with you.

Again, if possible, get my **Where to Get the Money Now** System as I have everything done for you in a simple and easy to understand PowerPoint presentation that's been proven to work with students across the country. This is going to save you a bunch of time and energy, so you can just focus on meeting a ton of people and don't have to worry about putting together a system and presentation and paperwork, etc. I already did that for you. Use my knowledge and experience to make yourself money faster and easier. Speaking of faster and easier, you're going to love the next chapter about my private lender luncheon, so let's jump right into it!

CHAPTER 8

THE PRIVATE LENDER LUNCHEON

MANY, MANY YEARS AGO, BEFORE I got into real estate investing (Yes! This goes back a long time!), Carol Joy and I received a letter from a local estate planning attorney here in Morehead City, NC inviting me to something he called a luncheon. Basically, he invited us out to lunch at a nice restaurant, and he was going to give us some information about why we should have an estate plan or why we should have an attorney to do our estate planning for us.

We didn't really know much about it except that it was at a nice restaurant, we were going to get lunch, and we might learn a thing or two about estate planning, so even though we weren't really looking to hire an attorney at that point in time, it piqued our interest. Enough so that we thought, "hey, at least we'll get a nice meal out of it!" Since we didn't have anything else planned that day, we decided to go!

At the lunch, we learned some of the important questions that you should be asking yourself as it relates to estate planning, and we learned more about estate planning itself of course. I mean, that's why we were invited, right? But as I'm sitting there listening to the attorney speaking, I knew from the very beginning that this was nothing more than a very, very nice lead generating activity that the attorney was putting on.

Why was he buying us lunch? Because he wanted our business! Did it work? Well, ask me when you see me, and I'll tell you!

Let's fast forward a few years though, and when I started really focusing on attracting and raising private money, one thing that I've learned at the very beginning, is that if I go to chasing money, the money is going to elude me. And so, even from day one of attracting the money, I put on my education hat or my teacher hat. And I always frame myself as a teacher as related to private money because I knew it wasn't going to work if I asked people for money. I had to educate them on what private money was, along with how to use it along with Self-Directed IRA's.

Now the reason that having the teacher hat on works so well is because you're not coming across like you're selling. You're not coming across like a sales person. You're really enlightening people about what this world of private money is all about. So, remembering the event I attended to learn about estate planning, I decided that a great way to educate people about private money was to get them to come to a private lender luncheon! The private lender luncheon is an opportunity to teach. It's an opportunity to come to connect and to network, and that's why it works so well!

But also, another reason that I really like the Private Lender Luncheons is because it takes the same amount of time to teach one person about private money as you can teach 25 people about private money. In other words, you can get a bunch of potential private lenders together in one room and walk out with lots of cash for your deals. The private lender luncheon really lets you get your message out to a roomful of people in about the same amount of time it takes to get it out to just one, maximizing your time and putting your business into overdrive.

My goal at each event is to get pledges for $100,000 to $200,000 per entity in attendance, but I've leveraged the private lender luncheon in my own business for up to a million dollars per event before. You can too, but you've got to do it right. So, with that, let me share with you the secrets I've learned to putting together an event that will both wow your potential lenders AND get the cash flowing into your real estate business.

PRE-LUNCHEON

As the great Benjamin Franklin once said, "If you fail to plan, you plan to fail." So, the first part of having a private lender luncheon is to plan everything out. This is the most time intensive step because everything has to be set-up and ready to go. Do this part right, and the rest is easy!

Let's break this down into smaller steps to make sure that you've got everything you need to hold a successful luncheon yourself!

STEP 1. CHOOSE THE DATE AND LOCATION FOR YOUR LUNCHEON

You might not even know where you're having the luncheon, but setting the date is always the first step. Give yourself a deadline. I do this in all aspects of my business.

I may not have any idea how I'm going to pull something off, but giving myself a deadline drives me to start planning. Set a date no more than thirty days out. Thirty days is plenty of time to get everything in place and (if necessary) notify your current employer you'll be taking that day off.

And plan on hosting your event on Tuesday, Wednesday, Thursday, or Saturday. I've found that those are the best days to make sure you get as many people out as possible.

So, find a place that is open on one of those days and choose something that will be the nicest place you can afford. That means no Denny's or Golden Corral – even if you like those places. The best option is a local country club. If you're not a member of one, perhaps you have a friend or relative who could is a member and would be willing to help you. If this option is unavailable, the next best venue is the nicest hotel your budget will allow. It's got to be the best you can afford because you want to leave a good impression on people and show them that you're willing to make the right investments for your business.

Another acceptable option is a very nice restaurant. If you must go this route, be sure to book a private room, so there are no distractions. Don't let the expense scare you off – you're going to bring in lots of money for this, but only if you make the effort to do it right.

Obviously, lunch is on you – who can resist a nice lunch in a pleasant setting, especially when it's paid for by someone else? But it's very important that you choose the meal. Your guests will not be ordering off of a menu.

By the way, do you know that most mortgage brokers spend about $50-$100 on a good lead? If you talk to an attorney, it's not uncommon for them to spend between $100-$150 for a good lead. Even insurance agents spend $50-$100 on a good lead. So if you want to raise $100,000 or MORE, then do you think you should be willing to spend $50-$100 for someone's lunch?

Keep in mind that it all might sound like a lot of money (and it is) and when you put it in perspective, let's say you spend $50 per person for lunch and you get 20 people to show up. That's $1,000 you just spent on lunch – that you didn't even eat!!! WOW! Now out of 20 people, what if you got a verbal commitment from just 2 people at $100,000 or $200,000 or more each? How many deals can you do with $200,000 or more? How much money could you make? Was that worth it?

STEP 2. PUT YOUR GUEST LIST TOGETHER

How do you determine who's on the guest list? First, all guests will be from your warm market. A private lender luncheon is not effective for cold market lenders or folks you don't know.

Folks you invite CAN bring as guests' people you don't know yet, but these are referrals, not cold market lenders. Make a list of forty potential luncheon guests. If you've joined Business Networking International or the Rotary Club, the members of these organizations should be on your list. When inviting a married prospect, always include the spouse in your invitation.

Aside from invited guests, you'll have your team present: your CPA, real estate attorney, your Realtor(s), business partner(s), and sellers and buyers of properties you've purchased. In addition, if you have any, invite some of your current private lenders, including any who have pledged funds to you, even if you haven't actually used those funds yet. All these folks add credibility to you and your program and can help answer questions for you.

You know, it's always interesting to see who is talking to who. Some people won't feel comfortable asking me questions and instead will want to ask my realtor or attorney or even one of my private lenders. It's great to have them there, so they can help you get more money!

And hey, they get a free lunch, so you know why they're coming to help you!

Step 3. Pick Up The Phone And Call Your List

This is not a task you should delegate. Do not send out fancy, printed invitations. Two weeks before the luncheon, pick up the phone and start calling the invitees yourself.

On these invitation calls, do not discuss private lending or private lenders. Your conversation should be similar to the conversations you have when you share your 16-minute recording. It should go something like this:

'Hey, this is (your name).

How are you doing?

Great!

I'm putting on a very nice luncheon at (name of venue) on (date). I'd love for you to attend if you can.

I'll be putting on a presentation about how people can get higher rates of return on their investment capital and retirement accounts than they can get anywhere else, safely and securely. There's absolutely no obligation for you to engage after the luncheon, but I'd really like for you to come and support me in this effort.

I promise to have you in and out within an hour and fifteen minutes.

It would be great to get your feedback on my approach and hear how I can do it better in the future.'

Don't come across on this call like you're trying to talk anyone into anything. You're not chasing or begging. You're simply making a nice luncheon available, so that you can share some information about how to get unbelievable returns on investments.

If you think of someone a week before the luncheon or run into a prospective lender the day before the event, definitely invite them! I have received pledges from folks I invited to an event at the last minute. But the best strategy for inviting people is to give them two weeks' notice. Keep inviting prospects until you have twenty to twenty-five yeses.

In my **Where to Get the Money Now** system, I have bonus information on how to have a virtual assistant handle your invitations for you. I don't use this technique any more, but I've included it in the system for you if you decide you'd like to use it.

Step 4. Call The Invitees A Second Time

The day before your luncheon, you or your assistant will call the invitees and your team again. Tell them you need to confirm the number of attendees with the venue at which you're hosting the event. Also, ask if the invitees have any dietary restrictions.

I know from experience the importance of this confirmation phone call—most restaurants and clubs will let you give a final 24-hour notice on the head count—and this also reminds those who are attending and gets a double commitment from everyone involved. Then, call the venue with a final count and arrange to pay for the meal.

Step 5. Get Your Resources Together

Have extra copies of your 16-minute CD, the private lender brochure, and the interest-level form. Another thing you will want to provide at each table is a notepad and pen for each attendee. That way when you tell them to write something down that's especially important, they'll have something to write on.

During this entire time, there's one thing you should be doing regularly, and that's practicing your presentation! No one expects you to be a professional public speaker and blow them out of the water, and as my friend Chaffee-Thanh Nguyen says, "The quality of your life is based upon the quality of your communication." This means that the better you can present the presentation and convey your message of why they should be your private lender, the more money you're going to raise. So the key to your success here is practice, practice, practice!

Now, if you're just absolutely horrible at presenting or you get stage fright, you could have one of your team members do the presentation for you. And since you're the one that everyone is investing with, it's best if you can do it yourself. So the best thing to do is practice as much as possible and even practice in front of a couple of friends and ask for their feedback. The more you do it, the easier it will get, so just keep doing it over and over again. Its like anything you do. The more you do it, the easier it will get, so get to practicing right now!

And that's it for the planning stage!!! You're ready to go now! Hold your luncheon and get a lot of money! Easy peasy right? Stage 2 is the presentation itself.

THE LUNCHEON

At this point, you should have practiced your presentation like 100 times, right? So now you're an absolute pro at it, and you've memorized the entire thing! So maybe not yet, and you get my point... You're ready to go!

Before the presentation though you can do a few things.

STEP 1: WELCOME YOUR GUESTS

The first thing you should do is make sure you welcome all your guests!

Do a little bit of networking and show them where they can sit down for their lunch. Make sure some nice music is playing in the background and keep it nice and casual. Make them feel comfortable and welcome. Let them know when what's going to happen and when you'll be starting.

STEP 2: EAT UP

Next of course is lunch! Eat up! Sit down with your guests, and eat a bit of food. Then go around and see how everyone is doing. Not everyone will be done eating by the time you're ready to begin the presentation, but that's okay. Let them know that they can keep eating, and in order to respect everyone's time, you're going to get started.

STEP 3: PRESENTATION

Now if you have my **Where to Get the Money Now** system, I've already created your presentation for you. You just have to edit it here and there to put in your name and company, and you're done. If you don't have my system, then why not!?!? Ha! Seriously though, I covered your private money program in the previous chapter, so just make sure you have all the relevant information you need in your presentation that you've already practiced a 100 times, right?

PRO TIP

Here's a pro tip for you! Ask your team members questions throughout the presentation! For instance, you can ask your real estate attorney, "Are there any concerns a private lender should have?" He or she will answer that there are no concerns because private lenders are protected by receiving the mortgage, deed of trust, and promissory note, and that all documents are recorded. I ask my current private lenders to describe what their experience with me has been like. These third-party endorsements will reinforce the information you've just given your guests in the presentation.

STEP 4: WRAP IT UP

When you're done with the presentation and you've answered all the questions (or ran out of time), then I recommend you pass out a

Private Lending Brochure (which of course I've already made for you in my **Where to Get the Money Now** System).

And of course you've probably heard the saying, "The gold is in the follow-up!", so if your guest doesn't give you a verbal commitment right there and then, then see if they want to schedule a follow-up meeting with you and when. You can do this by talking to everyone individually or having them fill out a post-event assessment or questionnaire. And yep, you guessed it, it's already included in my **Where to Get the Money Now** System. I've made it nice and easy for you, so you don't have to waste any time doing it all yourself.... I've already done it for you!

Pro Tip

It's essential that you begin and end on time. No one will be willing to lend money to someone who comes across as disrespectful of others' time and schedules. Allow them to leave at the end of the ninety minutes but make sure they know that you'll hang around as long as they'd like, so that you can answer all their questions.

Post-Luncheon

So now that lunch is over, what should you do? Hope and pray that someone calls you and gives you money? Oh My Lands of course not!!! Within 24-48 hours after the luncheon, call every prospective lender who attended the event, regardless of the level of interest they expressed on their forms. This call must be from you, not your assistant.

There are three things you must do on this call:

1. Thank them for attending and supporting you at the luncheon.
2. Ask for their feedback. Ask them questions like:
   a. How do you think I did?
   b. Was the information clear?

    c. Do you have any suggestions about how I could do better?

3. Ask them if they have any questions.

    a. What questions can I answer for you about my program?

    b. Are there any clarifications I can give you?

    c. Do you want to continue letting the banks take advantage of you and your money or are you ready to start working with me now? (Ha! Just kidding on this one. This is a question might hit too close to home and offend someone instead of motivating them to work with you, so even if you're thinking it, don't ask it!)

And that's it! You're done! Pretty easy huh? Following this simple 3 Stage process, I've raised literally MILLIONS of dollars in private money, and you can too!!!

CHAPTER 9

TAP INTO THE POWER OF SELF-DIRECTED IRAS

WHEN MOST PEOPLE THINK ABOUT retirement, they think 401k, Pension plan, Social Security, and IRA. If someone has been working in a company, they probably know about these retirement vehicles, and a lot of people might have already put money into one or more of these tools. What they probably don't know though is that with a specific type of IRA, they can lend out their money and make more money or they can use their retirement funds to buy real estate, businesses, precious metals, and more! We call this a Self-Directed IRA.

Now this isn't an IRA at your local brokerage company like Charles Schwab or Fidelity or something. These are special IRAs, with special companies that act as "custodians" of your money. There's only a handful of them across the country, and when you know how to use them, they can provide you with an unlimited supply of private money you can use for your deals!

In the words of Kathy Fettke, Co-CEO and Co-Founder of RealWealth, "A self-directed Individual Retirement Arrangement (IRA) is an individual retirement account that allows the account owner to direct the account trustee to make a broader range of investments beyond stocks and bonds, including: real estate, franchises, precious metals, and private equity. Internal Revenue Service (IRS) regulations require that either a qualified trustee, or custodian, hold the IRA assets on behalf of the IRA owner."

Did you get that? It's an IRA where the account owner (this would be your private lender) directs (or tells) the account trustee (the Self-Directed IRA company rep) to make a broader range of investments beyond stocks (i.e. your real estate deals!). You can't do this with Fidelity or Edward Jones or something. You have to do this through an IRS approved custodian or trustee.

Most people have no clue that this money is available to them to invest with you through a Self-Directed IRAs, so it's your job to educate them on how they can use it to fund your deals and get huge returns for themselves. Of course, if you want to educated someone on how to use Self-Directed IRA's, you have to understand them yourself, so I'm going to walk you through step-by-step on how to use Self-Directed IRA's to fund all your deals! In fact, I'm going to share with you the exact step-by-step process I personally use in my business to turn IRA funds into private money.

And let me tell you why this is so important for you to understand and share. Over fifty percent of our private lenders are funding our deals using Self-Directed IRAs. But before they had heard of my program, one hundred percent of them had never even heard of Self-Directed IRAs! If you don't understand and share the facts about this investment vehicle, you're leaving about half the money available to you on the table!

I want to keep it simple and easy for the private lender to do business with me, and I want the private lender to have to do as little as possible, so let me give you a big picture view of the entire process, so you can explain it to them. There's a handful of steps, so let's get started.

PRIVATE LENDER SETUP

Before you can get money for a deal, you have to make sure your private lender has their money in a Self-Directed IRA and it's ready to go when you find a deal. The first step to getting this done though has nothing to do with the private lender. Instead, it's about you and a self-directed IRA representative.

PRIVATE LENDER SETUP

1	2	3	4
Connect with a Self-Directed IRA Representative	Introduce Your Private Lender & Representative	Get Authorization for Rep to Acquire Lender's IRA Funds	Get Funded & Put the Money to Work in Deals

STEP 1: ESTABLISH A RELATIONSHIP WITH A SELF-DIRECTED IRA REP

If you're not sure who to contact or how, just reach out to my team, and we'll be glad to help. When you get the information on the company, call and tell them you want someone to whom you can refer all of your private lenders. Ask them to send some nice, classy brochures that you can hand out to all your prospective private lenders.

When you're one of my students, I've already done this step for you. I have a special relationship with a Self-Directed IRA company, and a special email and dedicated representatives are set up just for me and my students. If you're not one of my students yet, you'll have to do this step yourself.

STEP 2: PRIVATE LENDER MEETS SELF-DIRECTED IRA REP

Ask the private lender if they want you to set up a three-way introductory phone call between the lender, the Self-Directed IRA rep, and you, or if they would prefer to have the rep just call them directly. If they decide on the three-way call, you'll set it up and initiate it. You're in charge of the call.

Of course, you'll exchange pleasantries, and then have the rep explain how they'll carry out the done-for-you process. The rep will give an overview of how, in a done-for-you way, the private lender's funds will be transferred to the Self-Directed IRA account. The emphasis of the explanation will be on the fact the lender has to sign only one document to move the funds. I want the private lender to know how easy this process is going to be.

After signing one document, the private lender never has to talk to or call anyone to facilitate the process. After this step, the private lender will not have to do another thing until way down in the process.

STEP 3: AUTHORIZATION

Your Self-Directed IRA rep will email an authorization to your private lender for them to sign. That will allow the rep to act on their behalf to get their funds transferred from their current IRA to their Self-Directed IRA funded. Your private lender signs the authorization and sends it back to the rep.

It's important that the private lender follow up with their original plan administrator or the company that currently has the funds.

Sometimes the process can drag out, but both you and your private lender want this done as quickly as possible, so stay on top of your private lender to stay on top of the Self-Directed IRA rep to get this done.

Step 4: Get Funded

The Self-Directed IRA is now funded; the rep will notify you that the money has been transferred.

Now that the money is in the Self-Directed IRA and ready to be sent out to you, it's go time! We'll talk about that next and make sure you allow for about a month to get everything done. I've seen it happen in two weeks, and sometimes it's taken as long as eight weeks, but generally, it should happen in about a month. As I said earlier, the main thing is to be in communication with your private lender and encourage them to follow up with their plan administrator where the funds are currently.

Remember what comes first? THE MONEY! Do not make an offer on a property without the money for the deal being in place.

Find A Deal

Now that the money is in place, then you've got to find a deal! Once you do, that's when the excitement begins!

FIND A DEAL

1. Tell Your Private Lender Your Deal is a Go
2. Contact Your Real Estate Attorney or Closing Agent
3. Contact Your Self-Directed IRA Representative
4. Email Direction of Investment Letter to Your Lender

STEP 1: LET THE PRIVATE LENDER KNOW IT'S A GO!

Call the private lender and tell them the four things they want to know

1. The property's After Repair Value
2. The property's Location
3. The funding for the deal required from their IRA account
4. When the deal is going to close (in other words, when do the funds need to be there)

Let them know that you're going to be sending them a Direction of Investment letter for their signature after you get the mortgage and promissory note from your attorney. They're going to need to sign it and get it back to the Self-Directed IRA rep. You'll communicate most of these things to the private lender on the first deal only. After that, all they'll want to know is how much money you need and when.

STEP 2: CONTACT YOUR REAL ESTATE ATTORNEY

Have them prepare the closing agent instructions. They're going to need some information from you though:

1. The lender (in this case, the Self-Directed IRA company) and its address
2. Your private lender's name or Self-Directed IRA account number
3. What position the private lender is in (first position, second position, etc.)
4. The amount of the principal
5. The address of the property securing the note
6. The rate of interest and when payment of interest begins
7. The term
8. The frequency of payments

With this information, they can prepare the documents you need:

1. The promissory note
2. The mortgage

Do not... I repeat, do not attempt to create these documents yourself. You are not (well, most of my students are not) an attorney, and you do not want to take on this liability for yourself or the private lender. Find a good attorney you can trust and work with them to draw everything up. Tell them you're going to send them all your deals, so they give you a good price for your paperwork and closings; build a relationship with them. I've been with my same attorney since 2003! She knows exactly what I want and how to get everything done! So don't try to save a buck and do this yourself. A good attorney will pay for themselves many times over and save your behind at the same time!

Once they're done preparing these documents for you, have them send YOU the documents. You don't want them going anywhere else just yet because you must proofread them for accuracy.

In my experience, about nine out of ten documents sent to me by my real estate attorney has some inaccuracy in it, so this is a very important step. Make sure the information on the promissory note and the mortgage match.

"But Jay! I don't know how to read legal documents! How do I know if they're accurate or not?"

All you have to do is look at the email you sent your real estate attorney, check the information in it, and be sure what's on the promissory note and the mortgage match what you sent and that they match each other. Simple enough, and it's always better to be safe than sorry.

STEP 3: CONTACT THE SELF-DIRECTED IRA REP

Once you have the completed mortgage and the promissory note, send it over to your Self-Directed IRA rep and ask him or her to prepare the Direction of Investment (DOI). I've added this document in the Appendix of this book in case you wanted to see what it looks like.

The Direction of Investment document authorizes the Self-Directed IRA company to wire the funds to your real estate attorney's trust account for closing. Make sure you include the instructions for the wiring of the money when you send over the documents.

The information on DOI must match the information the mortgage and promissory note, and it must be signed by the private lender. It's very important to allow your Self-Directed IRA rep to complete this form. Every time I tried it, I messed it up! And you don't want your private lender trying to do it because it needs to be done correctly. Any discrepancies between the promissory note and the mortgage documents and the DOI only slows up the process. The Self-Directed IRA company will know exactly how to handle it, so let them do it!

Always mark the box of the front page of the DOI indicating you want expedited processing service. Expedited processing gets the funds into real estate attorney's trust account within 48 hours, and sometimes as little as 24, hours. If the private lender wants you to pay it, don't quibble. It's a small fee, and you never want to lose a deal over a few dollars.

STEP 4: EMAIL THE DIRECTION OF INVESTMENT TO YOUR PRIVATE LENDER

Your Self-Directed IRA rep will now email the Direction of Investment to your private lender for his or her signature and have them send it back to the Self-Directed IRA rep.

Notice that this is the first time the private lender has been directly involved in the process since setting everything up. The main reason is that they just don't care how the sausage is made so to say. They want to sign a form and get a big return on their money, so we keep it simple for them.

Speaking of which, there are only three things for the private lender to do throughout this entire process

1. Meet your Self-Directed IRA rep
2. Sign the authorization to fund the account
3. Sign the Direction of Investment

And they only have to do the first two things on their first deal with you. After that, the only thing they need to do is sign the DOI and cash their checks!

Once the Self-Directed IRA rep receives the SIGNED DOI from the private lender, they will process it and schedule the wiring of the funds to the closing agent. Now we're ready to close the deal!

CLOSE THE DEAL AND GET PAID

At the scheduled time, close the deal at your real estate attorney's office! And you're done! Pretty neat right?

CLOSE THE DEAL

Close the Deal　　　　　**Get Paid**

While there can be delays in the process due to all the moving parts, everything can be done in 7-14 days! The better your relationship with your real estate attorney and your private lender, the faster the whole thing will move along.

There is one exception to the above process though. This happens when the private lender establishes a Limited Liability Company (LLC), which makes them the custodian of their own retirement account and gives them check writing privileges on the account. If your private lender already has one of these, that's fine; you just deal directly with them, instead of having them establish a Self-Directed IRA account as described above, and they wire you the funds themselves.

However, if they do not already have this type of LLC and they bring up establishing one for purposes of doing business with you, I recommend you discourage it. It's very close to self-dealing, which is not allowed by the IRS. If the private lender wants more information about this, just refer to them to your Self-Directed IRA rep, so that they can get more information.

Notice how easy we've made this process for the private lender! After the first deal, they only have to sign a form and send it to the Self-Directed IRA rep. Nice and simple. Think about it. They set up an account at a Self-Directed IRA company, have someone do all the work to find and process a deal, give the borrower some funds, then sit back and let the big returns roll in! It's another win-win deal for everyone!

CHAPTER 10

A Business You Can Be Proud Of

CONGRATULATIONS! YOU NOW KNOW EVERYTHING you need to know to run your very own successful, very profitable real estate investment business. If you follow the program I've revealed in this book, you will attract millions of dollars in private money to fund all the deals you can handle.

But there's more to life than making money, and there's more to business than profits and bottom lines. You don't just want a business that pays the bills. You want a business you can be proud of. One that comes from running your business with character and integrity.

In my time on this earth, I've been blessed to learn many invaluable lessons that have helped make me the man I am today. Of all those lessons, though, I think what has resonated the most with me, and most shaped my life and work, was what I learned from a dear family friend, Miss Beulah Raynor.

Miss Beulah was an English professor at Wake Forest University. She taught my father freshman English way back in 1953. She was known around campus as one of the most challenging professors on staff, but my father quickly took a liking to her teaching style. Miss Beulah was demanding, yet kind-hearted. She and my father grew close, my father eventually working for her husband as a teaching assistant. Through the years, Miss Beulah stayed in touch with my father and became a close family friend.

When it came time for me to choose a college to attend, my father made one thing very clear. He told me, "You can attend any university you choose, but if I'm paying for it, it's going to be Wake Forest." Needless to say, the following fall I enrolled in Wake and was immediately "adopted" by Miss Beulah.

Her house was located right on campus, so I spent a great deal of time there. I ate Sunday dinner with her family, got help with my homework, and engaged in many discussions on a wide variety of topics. I knew I could always count on Miss Beulah giving me completely honest advice when it came to school, life, even relationships. She had a way of telling you truth that you didn't want to hear in a way that was loving and compassionate.

We lost Miss Beulah several years back. She was 101! I never will forget those dinners, those conversations, those lessons that helped mold a young, immature boy into a thriving, fulfilled adult. Miss Beulah was truly an inspiration.

Her view of life was that, regardless of what she was doing at any given moment, it was absolutely the best she'd ever experienced. If she was drinking a cup of coffee, it was the best coffee she'd ever tasted.

If friends stopped by for a visit, it was the most enjoyable visit she'd ever had. For her, each day, each moment, was a blessing and a joy. I couldn't help but be influenced by the spirit and example of this amazing woman.

Miss Beulah's philosophy of life consisted of three pillars. These three concepts became the foundation of my personal and professional life. I seek to put them into practice into all my relationships, whether in my family, my business, or my church. I'd like to share them with you, so that you might consider them as pillars of your own life and business.

First, don't judge others. Instead, always give them the benefit of the doubt.

Recently, I had referred to me a couple that, to many, would have appeared to be "not your typical buyer." They were a younger couple, with multiple tattoos and piercings. Without hesitation, I took them on as home buyers in my rent-to-own program, and quickly discovered how genuine and good-hearted they were. It's nearly impossible to judge a book by its cover, so I do my best to find out who a person is, rather than settle for assumptions based on how they look.

Second, trust everyone (until they give you a reason not to).

My very first private lender was a man that didn't appear to have more than a few dollars to his name. When he told me he had $125,000 to invest in a property, I didn't hesitate. The day I needed his check, I called him, and it was taken care of. I used that money for a successful deal. Thankfully that kind of trust has allowed me to continue in this business and enjoy great success. Always make sure you take another person at his or her word until they give you a good reason why you shouldn't.

Third, expect things to work out for the best, regardless of circumstances.

When I hire someone new, I expect individual to contribute to the welfare and prosperity of my business. When I invest in a house, I expect that the deal is going to work out and earn a profit for me. Obviously, the world isn't perfect. Everything won't go right all the time, but if you never take a chance, you never reap life's rewards. All too often I see investors who are afraid to "pull the trigger" and make a decision due to fear. Adopting Miss Beulah's optimistic philosophy in life helps dissolve such fear and give you confidence in the decisions you have to make as an entrepreneur.

I encourage you to think carefully about the attitudes I've shared with you above, and to apply them in your own life. See what kinds of changes begin to occur – witness new blessings in your life, family, business, and relationships. As I said before, I would not be the man I am today without the friendship and insight of Beulah Raynor. If I can model and pass on her wisdom so that others can be equally blessed, I will consider my life to be a success.

But isn't implementing this kind of profound thinking and behavior a challenge? It sure is! How is a person supposed to create such fundamental change? We often think to ourselves, "I'd really make some big changes if I only had the time." Sound familiar?

But what would you think if I told you that you can get a big start on positive, successful thinking and living in the first six minutes of your day? Everyone's got six minutes, right? Now, you're probably thinking, "What on earth could I accomplish in the just six minutes that would be able to affect my life so deeply?'

Let me share some principles that I learned from Hal Elrod's book *The Miracle Morning*. In that outstanding book, Elrod provides techniques that can, in just a short time, really make a difference in your mindset and behavior. Put them into practice, and you'll see a real transformation in your life.

In the first minute of your daily six-minute routine, just be silent. Use this minute to collect your thoughts and prepare for the day ahead. Pray, meditate, just count your breaths and calm your body and mind. I promise you, it'll do wonders!

In the second minute of your day, say affirmations you've composed to put yourself in a positive frame of mind. Saying, thinking about, and feeling these affirmations will help you begin to recognize, realize, and maximize your unlimited potential. During this time, you can also focus on the day's priorities and think of positive ways you can go about addressing them.

In the third minute of your routine, visualize the day ahead. Prepare yourself mentally for success Think about smiling or laughing with loved ones. Visualize positive, productive activities at your job or around your home. This will get you started off on the right foot and keep you in an optimistic frame of mind throughout your day.

For the rest of the six-minute routine, and lots of other great tips to becoming your very best self, go grab a copy of Hal Eldrod's *The Miracle Morning* for yourself. There's tons of great information in it. In fact, I would love to discuss it with you when you attend my Private Money Academy Conference. Remember, as a bonus for picking up this book, I've offered you free tickets to the event. Simply go to http://www.JayConner.com/Conference and get yourself registered for it today. This is a $2,995 value, so take advantage of it and come on out and let me know how you love my book and are using it to raise millions in private money!

CHAPTER 11

IT'S GO TIME!

S O THERE YOU HAVE IT – now you know all my secrets, including the philosophies that have built the pillars of my life and business! Now, all you have to do is sit back and wait for the money to start rolling in... right? Uh, wrong.

The tools, tips, and tricks I've given you in this book are the very ones I've used since the very beginning, and continue to use— every day—to build a thriving business. Alongside the pillars of God, church, family, and friends, I've been blessed to through real estate investment with private money to create a life I truly love. You can do the same, but let's put the emphasis where it needs to be... on the word "do." The bridge between knowledge and success is ACTION!

But chances are pretty good that you've got some butterflies fluttering around in your stomach at the thought of all this – approaching potential private lenders, putting on luncheons, purchasing real estate... it all sounds so scary! And you know what? That's perfectly normal! All of us—myself included—are scared when doing something new. Remember, the beginning of a journey is often times lonely and scary, but the difference between those who build the life of their dreams and those who don't is one thing, "Action." It's not luck, DNA, education, privilege, or any other factor other than ACTION. How do you overcome fear? By taking action!

See, most folks get this all backward – they think that, when you fear doing something, the answer is to get information. They believe that at some point you can get enough information to remove your fear, then you're cleared to act. In reality, it's just the opposite. Of course, information is essential. We never want to jump into something blindly and foolishly. But most people get stuck in the information-gathering stage and never get out of neutral. They're kept from success by "analysis paralysis."

Well, I think you'll agree that I've given you all the information you need to get started and to flourish in your real estate investment business. You've got the facts – now it's time to put them to work. You'll find, as all successful people do, that putting your knowledge to work is the only answer to overcoming your fear. And remember: "successful people get comfortable being uncomfortable.'

Let me explain what I mean. At the beginning of my live events, I'll hold up a $100 bill in front of the room. Then I'll simply say, "Who would like this $100 bill?" Usually, a lot of hands go up, and I just stand there smiling and waiting. Eventually, someone will stand up, run to the front of the room, and take the bill out of my hand, before returning to their seat.

Then, I'll ask the audience, "What did this person do that nobody else did?" The answer is, they got off their butt and took action. They did what was necessary to get the money. It's such a simple demonstration, but it communicates so much about what you must do if you want to succeed in life.

The next question I ask the audience is, "How many of y'all thought about getting up and taking the money from me, but stopped yourself?"

And then, "What was it you told yourself that stopped you from getting up out of your chair?"

I get a lot of common answers, "I didn't want to look like I needed the money." "I wasn't sure you'd give it to me if I came up there." "I was too far back in the room." "I didn't want to seem greedy." "I was waiting for further instructions."

And the one that really gets me, "I've been to your live events before, and I knew what you were going to do. I didn't want to take advantage of that knowledge." Are you kidding? Would you spend thousands of dollars on real estate education and then not use what you know to succeed?

In the end, there's a universal truth from this story, that how you do anything is how you do everything. If you're cautious about coming to get the $100 bill out of my hand, you're probably cautious about everything you do. Likewise, if you hold yourself back out of the fear of looking foolish, you'll probably hold yourself back from looking foolish in everything you do.

I'm speaking from experience because I was like the member of the audience willing to risk looking like a fool -- and it saved my business. Before I knew anything about private money, I funded my real estate deals with lines of credit at the bank. In the fall of 2008, when we had the global financial crisis, I was cut off from the banks with no notice. I had deals under contract and no way to fund them. When I had that fateful conversation with my banker, I realized I had just two choices:

to do nothing (inaction is a decision) or to continue looking for a way to fix my problem.

I chose to keep looking. My first action was asking other real estate investor friends how they fund their deals when they're not using a bank. Thankfully, one of my friends told me that Ron LeGrand funded his deals with private money, so I made the decision to attend Ron LeGrand's "Quick Start Real Estate School." I learned about private money and took massive action. Within 90 days, I'd raised $2,150,000 in private money. Where would I have been if I hadn't taken action? Out of business.

In my observation, the most important thing that separates winners from losers is taking action. Winners simply get up and do what's got to be done – in spite of their fears, their insecurities, their ignorance, or their lack of clarity. Once you develop a plan, get started and don't delay. Winners take massive action.

The cool thing about taking action is, when you actually do it, you start triggering all kinds of other outcomes that will carry you forward to success. In fact, just acting on your goals tells the people around you that you're serious in your intentions. It makes others perceive you differently when you act – and believe it or not, people who take action are actually in the minority, so you'll earn a lot of respect.

And there's one other thing you can do in order to help you in your action taking activities, and that's to schedule them out. I've been in and around business for a long time, and one of the most important lessons I've learned is that "all successes are scheduled." In other words, you won't just "happen" to raise private money, put on a successful private lender luncheon, or rehab and sell a home for a big profit.

These things are never accidental – they will happen because you put the necessary activities into your calendar and committed to making them happen. So get out your phone or paper calendar and pen, start scheduling your successes right now, and go take massive action!

I'm going to leave you with this final thought… In 2017 we lost one of my generation's most beloved celebrities – David Cassidy. I grew up listening to his music and spent many hours watching him on TV as part of The Partridge Family. From all appearances, David Cassidy lived a full and interesting life, but it was widely reported that as he lay dying, his last words were, "So much wasted time.'

Is that what you want to be the dominant thought at the end of your life? Do you want regrets over the things you could have done, the experiences you could have had, the fulfillment you could have enjoyed? Or do you want to be able to look back over your life and know that you got out of each day—each and every moment—the most you could?

It's time to get started – your amazing journey awaits… and I'm so thankful that you chose to use this book as your map and me as your guide. I appreciate you and wish you the best of luck on your journey as you go out there and raise millions of dollars in private money. I'm looking forward to seeing you at my next Private Money Academy Conference where we can talk all about your successes in this business.

I'm Jay Conner, The Private Money Authority. Wishing you all the best, and here's to taking your real estate investing business to the next level. I'll see you on the inside. Bye for now.

APPENDIX:

SAMPLE DOCUMENTS

SAMPLE PURCHASE CONTRACT

OFFER TO PURCHASE AND CONTRACT
[Consult "Guidelines" (Form 2G) for guidance in completing this form]

For valuable consideration, the receipt and legal sufficiency of which are hereby acknowledged, Buyer offers to purchase and Seller upon acceptance agrees to sell and convey the Property on the terms and conditions of this Offer To Purchase and Contract and any addendum or modification made in accordance with its terms (together the "Contract").

1. **TERMS AND DEFINITIONS:** The terms listed below shall have the respective meaning given them as set forth adjacent to each term.

(a) **"Seller":** _____

(b) **"Buyer":** _____

(c) **"Property":** The Property shall include all that real estate described below together with all appurtenances thereto including the improvements located thereon and the fixtures and personal property listed in Paragraphs 2 and 3 below.

> NOTE: If the Property will include a manufactured (mobile) home(s), Buyer and Seller should consider including the Manufactured (Mobile) Home provision in the Additional Provisions Addendum (Standard Form 2A11-T) with this offer.

Street Address: _____
City: _____ Zip: _____
County: _____ , North Carolina

> NOTE: Governmental authority over taxes, zoning, school districts, utilities and mail delivery may differ from address shown.

Legal Description: (Complete *ALL* applicable)
Plat Reference: Lot/Unit _____ , Block/Section _____ , Subdivision/Condominium _____
_____ , as shown on Plat Book/Slide _____ at Page(s) _____
The PIN/PID or other identification number of the Property is: _____
Other description: _____
Some or all of the Property may be described in Deed Book _____ at Page _____

(d) **"Purchase Price":**

$ _____	paid in U.S. Dollars upon the following terms:
$ _____	BY DUE DILIGENCE FEE made payable and delivered to Seller by the Effective Date.
$ _____	BY INITIAL EARNEST MONEY DEPOSIT made payable and delivered to Escrow Agent named in Paragraph 1(f) by ☐ cash ☐ personal check ☐ official bank check ☐ wire transfer, ☐ electronic transfer, EITHER ☐ with this offer OR ☐ within five (5) days of the Effective Date of this Contract.
$ _____	BY (ADDITIONAL) EARNEST MONEY DEPOSIT made payable and delivered to Escrow Agent named in Paragraph 1(f) by cash, official bank check, wire transfer or electronic transfer no later than 5 p.m. on _____ , TIME BEING OF THE ESSENCE.
$ _____	BY ASSUMPTION of the unpaid principal balance and all obligations of Seller on the existing loan(s) secured by a deed of trust on the Property in accordance with the attached Loan Assumption Addendum (Standard Form 2A6-T).
$ _____	BY SELLER FINANCING in accordance with the attached Seller Financing Addendum (Standard Form 2A5-T).
$ _____	BY BUILDING DEPOSIT in accordance with the attached New Construction Addendum (Standard Form 2A3-T).
$ _____	BALANCE of the Purchase Price in cash at Settlement (some or all of which may be paid with the proceeds of a new loan).

Should Buyer fail to deliver either the Due Diligence Fee or any Initial Earnest Money Deposit by their due dates, or should any check or other funds paid by Buyer be dishonored, for any reason, by the institution upon which the payment is drawn, Buyer shall have one (1) banking day after written notice to deliver cash, official bank check, wire transfer or electronic transfer to the payee. In the event Buyer does not timely deliver the required funds, Seller shall have the right to terminate this Contract upon written notice to Buyer.

Page 1 of 14

This form jointly approved by:
North Carolina Bar Association
North Carolina Association of REALTORS®, Inc.

STANDARD FORM 2-T
Revised 7/2019
© 7/2019

Buyer's initials _____   Seller's initials _____

Dream Maker Properties, LLC, 111 Cloister Court, Ste. 214 Chapel Hill NC 27514   Phone (919)932-9623   Fax (919)932-9623   0001
R. Allen Lyles   Produced with zipForm® by zipLogix 18070 Fifteen Mile Road, Fraser, Michigan 48026   www.zipLogix.com

Get Your Private Money Event Ticket - www.JayConner.com/conference

(e) **"Earnest Money Deposit"**: The Initial Earnest Money Deposit, the Additional Earnest Money Deposit and any other earnest monies paid or required to be paid in connection with this transaction, collectively the "Earnest Money Deposit", shall be deposited and held in escrow by Escrow Agent until Closing, at which time it will be credited to Buyer, or until this Contract is otherwise terminated. In the event: (1) this offer is not accepted; or (2) a condition of any resulting contract is not satisfied, then the Earnest Money Deposit shall be refunded to Buyer. In the event of breach of this Contract by Seller, the Earnest Money Deposit shall be refunded to Buyer upon Buyer's request, but such return shall not affect any other remedies available to Buyer for such breach. In the event of breach of this Contract by Buyer, the Earnest Money Deposit shall be paid to Seller. The payment of the Earnest Money Deposit to Seller and the retention of any Due Diligence Fee by Seller (without regard to their respective amounts, including zero) together shall serve as liquidated damages ("Liquidated Damages") and as Seller's sole and exclusive remedy for such breach, but without limiting Seller's rights under Paragraphs 4(d) and 4(e) for damage to the Property. It is acknowledged by the parties that the amount of the Liquidated Damages is compensatory and not punitive, such amount being a reasonable estimation of the actual loss that Seller would incur as a result of a breach of this Contract by Buyer. The payment to Seller and/or retention by Seller of the Liquidated Damages shall not constitute a penalty or forfeiture but actual compensation for Seller's anticipated loss, both parties acknowledging the difficulty determining Seller's actual damages for such breach. If legal proceedings are brought by Buyer or Seller against the other to recover the Earnest Money Deposit, the prevailing party in the proceeding shall be entitled to recover from the non-prevailing party reasonable attorney fees and court costs incurred in connection with the proceeding.

(f) **"Escrow Agent"** (insert name): _____

> NOTE: In the event of a dispute between Seller and Buyer over the disposition of the Earnest Money Deposit held in escrow, a licensed real estate broker ("Broker") is required by state law (and Escrow Agent, if not a Broker, hereby agrees) to retain the Earnest Money Deposit in the Escrow Agent's trust or escrow account until Escrow Agent has obtained a written release from the parties consenting to its disposition or until disbursement is ordered by a court of competent jurisdiction. Alternatively, if a Broker or an attorney licensed to practice law in North Carolina ("Attorney") is holding the Earnest Money Deposit, the Broker or Attorney may deposit the disputed monies with the appropriate clerk of court in accordance with the provisions of N.C.G.S. §93A-12.

THE PARTIES AGREE THAT A REAL ESTATE BROKERAGE FIRM ACTING AS ESCROW AGENT MAY PLACE THE EARNEST MONEY DEPOSIT IN AN INTEREST BEARING TRUST ACCOUNT AND THAT ANY INTEREST EARNED THEREON SHALL BE DISBURSED TO THE ESCROW AGENT MONTHLY IN CONSIDERATION OF THE EXPENSES INCURRED BY MAINTAINING SUCH ACCOUNT AND RECORDS ASSOCIATED THEREWITH.

(g) **"Effective Date"**: The date that: (1) the last one of Buyer and Seller has signed or initialed this offer or the final counteroffer, if any, and (2) such signing or initialing is communicated to the party making the offer or counteroffer, as the case may be. The parties acknowledge and agree that the initials lines at the bottom of each page of this Contract are merely evidence of their having reviewed the terms of each page, and that the complete execution of such initials lines shall not be a condition of the effectiveness of this Agreement.

(h) **"Due Diligence"**: Buyer's opportunity to investigate the Property and the transaction contemplated by this Contract, including but not necessarily limited to the matters described in Paragraph 4 below, to decide whether Buyer, in Buyer's sole discretion, will proceed with or terminate the transaction.

(i) **"Due Diligence Fee"**: A negotiated amount, if any, paid by Buyer to Seller with this Contract for Buyer's right to terminate the Contract for any reason or no reason during the Due Diligence Period. It shall be the property of Seller upon the Effective Date and shall be a credit to Buyer at Closing. The Due Diligence Fee shall be non-refundable except in the event of a material breach of this Contract by Seller, or if this Contract is terminated under Paragraph 8(n) or as otherwise provided in any addendum hereto. Buyer and Seller each expressly waive any right that they may have to deny the right to conduct Due Diligence or to assert any defense as to the enforceability of this Contract based on the absence or alleged insufficiency of any Due Diligence Fee, it being the intent of the parties to create a legally binding contract for the purchase and sale of the Property without regard to the existence or amount of any Due Diligence Fee.

(j) **"Due Diligence Period"**: The period beginning on the Effective Date and extending through 5:00 p.m. on _____ *TIME BEING OF THE ESSENCE*.

(k) **"Settlement"**: The proper execution and delivery to the closing attorney of all documents necessary to complete the transaction contemplated by this Contract, including the deed, settlement statement, deed of trust and other loan or conveyance documents, and the closing attorney's receipt of all funds necessary to complete such transaction.

(l) **"Settlement Date"**: The parties agree that Settlement will take place on _____ (the "Settlement Date"), unless otherwise agreed in writing, at a time and place designated by Buyer.

Page 2 of 14

Buyer's initials _____ Seller's initials _____

Produced with zipForm® by zipLogix 18070 Fifteen Mile Road, Fraser, Michigan 48026 www.zipLogix.com 0001

(m) **"Closing"**: The completion of the legal process which results in the transfer of title to the Property from Seller to Buyer, which includes the following steps: (1) the Settlement (defined above); (2) the completion of a satisfactory title update to the Property following the Settlement; (3) the closing attorney's receipt of authorization to disburse all necessary funds; and (4) recordation in the appropriate county registry of the deed(s) and deed(s) of trust, if any, which shall take place as soon as reasonably possible for the closing attorney after Settlement. Upon Closing, the proceeds of sale shall be disbursed by the closing attorney in accordance with the settlement statement and the provisions of Chapter 45A of the North Carolina General Statutes. If the title update should reveal unexpected liens, encumbrances or other title defects, or if the closing attorney is not authorized to disburse all necessary funds, then the Closing shall be suspended and the Settlement deemed delayed under Paragraph 12 (Delay in Settlement/Closing).

WARNING: The North Carolina State Bar has determined that the performance of most acts and services required for a closing constitutes the practice of law and must be performed only by an attorney licensed to practice law in North Carolina. State law prohibits unlicensed individuals or firms from rendering legal services or advice. Although non-attorney settlement agents may perform limited services in connection with a closing, they may not perform all the acts and services required to complete a closing. A closing involves significant legal issues that should be handled by an attorney. Accordingly it is the position of the North Carolina Bar Association and the North Carolina Association of REALTORS® that all buyers should hire an attorney licensed in North Carolina to perform a closing.

(n) **"Special Assessments"**: A charge against the Property by a governmental authority in addition to ad valorem taxes and recurring governmental service fees levied with such taxes, or by an owners' association in addition to any regular assessment (dues), either of which may be a lien against the Property. A Special Assessment may be either proposed or confirmed.

"Proposed Special Assessment": A Special Assessment that is under formal consideration but which has not been approved prior to Settlement.

"Confirmed Special Assessment": A Special Assessment that has been approved prior to Settlement whether payable in a lump sum or future installments.

NOTE: Any Proposed and Confirmed Special Assessments must be identified by Seller in paragraph 7(c), and Buyer's and Seller's respective responsibilities for Proposed and Confirmed Special Assessments are addressed in paragraphs 6(a) and 8(k).

2. **FIXTURES AND EXCLUSIONS.**
(a) **Specified Items:** Unless identified in subparagraph (d) below, the following items, including all related equipment and remote control devices, if any, are deemed fixtures and shall convey, included in the Purchase Price free of liens:

- Alarm and security systems (attached) for security, fire, smoke, carbon monoxide or other toxins with all related access codes, sensors, cameras, dedicated monitors, hard drives, video recorders, power supplies and cables; doorbells/chimes
- All stoves/ranges/ovens; built-in appliances; attached microwave oven; vent hood
- Antennas; satellite dishes and receivers
- Basketball goals and play equipment (permanently attached or in-ground)
- Ceiling and wall-attached fans; light fixtures (including existing bulbs)
- Fireplace insert; gas logs or starters; attached fireplace screens; wood or coal stoves
- Floor coverings (attached)
- Fuel tank(s) whether attached or buried and including any contents that have not been used, removed or resold to the fuel provider as of Settlement. NOTE: Seller's use, removal or resale of fuel in any fuel tank is subject to Seller's obligation under Paragraph 8(c) to provide working, existing utilities through the earlier of Closing or possession by Buyer.
- Garage door openers with all controls

- Generators that are permanently wired
- Invisible fencing with power supply, controls and receivers
- Landscape and outdoor trees and plants (except in moveable containers); raised garden; landscape and foundation lighting; outdoor sound systems; permanent irrigation systems and controls; rain barrels; landscape water features; address markers
- Mailboxes; mounted package and newspaper receptacles
- Mirrors attached to walls, ceilings, cabinets or doors; all bathroom wall mirrors
- Storage shed; utility building
- Swimming pool (excluding inflatable); spa; hot tub
- Solar electric and solar water heating systems
- Sump-pumps, radon fans and crawl space ventilators; de-humidifiers that are permanently wired
- Surface-mounting brackets for television and speakers; recess-mounted speakers; mounted intercom system
- Water supply equipment, including filters, conditioning and softener systems; re-circulating pumps; well pumps and tanks
- Window/Door blinds and shades, curtain and drapery rods and brackets, door and window screens and combination doors, awnings and storm windows

Page 3 of 14

STANDARD FORM 2-T
Revised 7/2019
© 7/2019

Buyer's initials _____ Seller's initials _____

(b) **Items Leased or Not Owned:** Any item which is leased or not owned by Seller, such as fuel tanks, antennas, satellite dishes and receivers, appliances, and alarm and security systems must be identified here and shall not convey:

_____
_____
_____

(c) **Other Fixtures/Unspecified items:** Unless identified in subparagraph (d) below, any other item legally considered a fixture is included in the Purchase Price free of liens.

(d) **Other Items That Do Not Convey:** The following items shall not convey *(identify those items to be excluded under subparagraphs (a) and (c))*: _____
_____

Seller shall repair any damage caused by removal of any items excepted above.

3. **PERSONAL PROPERTY:** The following personal property shall be transferred to Buyer at no value at Closing: _____
_____

NOTE: Buyer is advised to consult with Buyer's lender to assure that the Personal Property items listed above can be included in this Contract.

4. **BUYER'S DUE DILIGENCE PROCESS:**

WARNING: BUYER IS STRONGLY ENCOURAGED TO CONDUCT DUE DILIGENCE DURING THE DUE DILIGENCE PERIOD. If Buyer is not satisfied with the results or progress of Buyer's Due Diligence, Buyer should terminate this Contract, PRIOR TO THE EXPIRATION OF THE DUE DILIGENCE PERIOD, unless Buyer can obtain a written extension from Seller. SELLER IS NOT OBLIGATED TO GRANT AN EXTENSION. Although Buyer may continue to investigate the Property following the expiration of the Due Diligence Period, Buyer's failure to deliver a Termination Notice to Seller prior to the expiration of the Due Diligence Period will constitute a waiver by Buyer of any right to terminate this Contract based on any matter relating to Buyer's Due Diligence. Provided however, following the Due Diligence Period, Buyer may still exercise a right to terminate if Seller fails to materially comply with any of Seller's obligations under Paragraph 8 of this Contract or for any other reason permitted under the terms of this Contract or North Carolina law.

(a) **Loan:** Buyer, at Buyer's expense, shall be entitled to pursue qualification for and approval of the Loan if any.

NOTE: Buyer's obligation to purchase the Property is not contingent on obtaining a Loan. Therefore, Buyer is advised to consult with Buyer's lender prior to signing this offer to assure that the Due Diligence Period allows sufficient time for the appraisal to be completed and for Buyer's lender to provide Buyer sufficient information to decide whether to proceed with or terminate the transaction.

(b) **Property Investigation:** Buyer or Buyer's agents or representatives, at Buyer's expense, shall be entitled to conduct all desired tests, surveys, appraisals, investigations, examinations and inspections of the Property as Buyer deems appropriate, including but NOT limited to the following:
  (i) **Inspections:** Inspections to determine the condition of any improvements on the Property, the presence of unusual drainage conditions or evidence of excessive moisture adversely affecting any improvements on the Property, the presence of asbestos or existing environmental contamination, evidence of wood-destroying insects or damage therefrom, and the presence and level of radon gas on the Property.
  (ii) **Review of Documents:** Review of the Declaration of Restrictive Covenants, Bylaws, Articles of Incorporation, Rules and Regulations, and other governing documents of any applicable owners' association and/or subdivision. If the Property is subject to regulation by an owners' association, it is recommended that Buyer review the completed Residential Property and Owners' Association Disclosure Statement provided by Seller prior to signing this offer. It is also recommended that the Buyer determine if the owners' association or its management company charges fees for providing information required by Buyer's lender or confirming restrictive covenant compliance.
  (iii) **Insurance:** Investigation of the availability and cost of insurance for the Property.
  (iv) **Appraisals:** An appraisal of the Property.
  (v) **Survey:** A survey to determine whether the property is suitable for Buyer's intended use and the location of easements, setbacks, property boundaries and other issues which may or may not constitute title defects.
  (vi) **Zoning and Governmental Regulation:** Investigation of current or proposed zoning or other governmental regulation that may affect Buyer's intended use of the Property, adjacent land uses, planned or proposed road construction, and school attendance zones.

Page 4 of 14

STANDARD FORM 2-T
Revised 7/2019
© 7/2019

Buyer's initials _____ Seller's initials _____

Produced with zipForm® by zipLogix 18070 Fifteen Mile Road, Fraser, Michigan 48026   www.zipLogix.com   0001

(vii) **Flood Hazard:** Investigation of potential flood hazards on the Property, and/or any requirement to purchase flood insurance in order to obtain the Loan.

(viii) **Utilities and Access:** Availability, quality, and obligations for maintenance of utilities including water, sewer, electric, gas, communication services, storm water management, and means of access to the Property and amenities.

(ix) **Streets/Roads:** Investigation of the status of the street/road upon which the Property fronts as well as any other street/road used to access the Property, including: (1) whether any street(s)/road(s) are public or private, (2) whether any street(s)/road(s) designated as public are accepted for maintenance by the State of NC or any municipality, or (3) if private or not accepted for public maintenance, the consequences and responsibility for maintenance and the existence, terms and funding of any maintenance agreements.

(x) **Fuel Tank:** Inspections to determine the existence, type and ownership of any fuel tank located on the Property.

> NOTE: Buyer is advised to consult with the owner of any leased fuel tank regarding the terms under which Buyer may lease the tank and obtain fuel.

(c) **Sale/Lease of Existing Property:** As noted in paragraph 5(b), unless otherwise provided in an addendum, this Contract is not conditioned upon the sale/lease or closing of other property owned by Buyer. Therefore, if Buyer must sell or lease other real property in order to qualify for a new loan or to otherwise complete the purchase of the Property, Buyer should seek to close on Buyer's other property prior to the end of the Due Diligence Period or be reasonably satisfied that closing on Buyer's other property will take place prior to the Settlement Date of this Contract.

(d) **Repair/Improvement Negotiations/Agreement:** Buyer acknowledges and understands that unless the parties agree otherwise, THE PROPERTY IS BEING SOLD IN ITS CURRENT CONDITION. Buyer and Seller acknowledge and understand that they may, but are not required to, engage in negotiations for repairs/improvements to the Property. Buyer is advised to make any repair/improvement requests in sufficient time to allow repair/improvement negotiations to be concluded prior to the expiration of the Due Diligence Period. Any agreement that the parties may reach with respect to repairs/improvements shall be considered an obligation of the parties and is an addition to this Contract and as such, must be in writing and signed by the parties in accordance with Paragraph 19.

> NOTE: See Paragraph 8(c), Access to Property and Paragraph 8(m), Negotiated Repairs/Improvements.

(e) **Buyer's Obligation to Repair Damage:** Buyer shall, at Buyer's expense, promptly repair any damage to the Property resulting from any activities of Buyer and Buyer's agents and contractors, but Buyer shall not be responsible for any damage caused by accepted practices either approved by the N.C. Home Inspector Licensure Board or applicable to any other N.C. licensed professional performing reasonable appraisals, tests, surveys, examinations and inspections of the Property. This repair obligation shall survive any termination of this Contract.

(f) **Indemnity:** Buyer will indemnify and hold Seller harmless from all loss, damage, claims, suits or costs, which shall arise out of any contract, agreement, or injury to any person or property as a result of any activities of Buyer and Buyer's agents and contractors relating to the Property except for any loss, damage, claim, suit or cost arising out of pre-existing conditions of the Property and/or out of Seller's negligence or willful acts or omissions. This indemnity shall survive this Contract and any termination hereof.

(g) **Buyer's Right to Terminate:** Buyer shall have the right to terminate this Contract for any reason or no reason, by delivering to Seller written notice of termination (the "Termination Notice") during the Due Diligence Period (or any agreed-upon written extension of the Due Diligence Period), *TIME BEING OF THE ESSENCE.* If Buyer timely delivers the Termination Notice, this Contract shall be terminated and the Earnest Money Deposit shall be refunded to Buyer.

(h) **CLOSING SHALL CONSTITUTE ACCEPTANCE OF THE PROPERTY IN ITS THEN EXISTING CONDITION UNLESS PROVISION IS OTHERWISE MADE IN WRITING.**

5. **BUYER REPRESENTATIONS:**
    (a) **Loan:** Buyer ☐ does ☐ does not intend to obtain a new loan in order to purchase the Property. If Buyer is obtaining a new loan, Buyer intends to obtain a loan as follows: ☐ FHA ☐ VA (attach FHA/VA Financing Addendum) ☐ Conventional ☐ Down Payment Assistance Program ☐ Other: _____ loan at a ☐ Fixed Rate ☐ Adjustable Rate in the principal amount of _____ plus any financed VA Funding Fee or FHA MIP for a term of _____ year(s), at an initial interest rate not to exceed _____ % per annum (the "Loan").

> NOTE: Buyer's obligations under this Contract are not conditioned upon obtaining or closing any loan. Some mortgage loan programs and Down Payment Assistance programs selected by Buyer may impose additional repair obligations, conditions or costs upon Seller or Buyer, and more information may be needed.

Page 5 of 14

STANDARD FORM 2-T
Revised 7/2019
© 7/2019

Buyer's initials _____ Seller's initials _____

NOTE: If Buyer does not intend to obtain a new loan, Seller is advised, prior to signing this offer, to obtain documentation from Buyer which demonstrates that Buyer will be able to close on the Property without the necessity of obtaining a new loan.

(b) **Other Property:** Buyer ☐ DOES ☐ DOES NOT have to sell or lease other real property in order to qualify for a new loan or to complete the purchase. *(Complete the following only if Buyer DOES have to sell or lease other real property:)*
Other Property Address: _____

☐ *(Check if applicable)* Buyer's other property IS under contract as of the date of this offer, and a copy of the contract has either been previously provided to Seller or accompanies this offer. *(Buyer may mark out any confidential information, such as the purchase price and the buyer's identity, prior to providing a copy of the contract to Seller.)* Failure to provide a copy of the contract shall not prevent this offer from becoming a binding contract; however, SELLER IS STRONGLY ENCOURAGED TO OBTAIN AND REVIEW THE CONTRACT ON BUYER'S PROPERTY PRIOR TO ACCEPTING THIS OFFER.

☐ *(Check if applicable)* Buyer's other property IS NOT under contract as of the date of this offer. Buyer's property *(check only ONE of the following options)*:
☐ is listed with and actively marketed by a licensed real estate broker.
☐ will be listed with and actively marketed by a licensed real estate broker.
☐ Buyer is attempting to sell/lease the Buyer's Property without the assistance of a licensed real estate broker.

NOTE: This Contract is NOT conditioned upon the sale/lease or closing of Buyer's other property. If the parties agree to make this Contract conditioned on a sale/lease or closing of Buyer's other property, an appropriate contingency addendum should be drafted by a North Carolina real estate attorney and added to this Contract.

(c) **Performance of Buyer's Financial Obligations:** To the best of Buyer's knowledge, there are no other circumstances or conditions existing as of the date of this offer that would prohibit Buyer from performing Buyer's financial obligations in accordance with this Contract, except as may be specifically set forth herein.

(d) **Residential Property and Owners' Association Property Disclosure Statement** *(check only one):*
☐ Buyer has received a signed copy of the N.C. Residential Property and Owners' Association Disclosure Statement prior to the signing of this offer.
☐ Buyer has NOT received a signed copy of the N.C. Residential Property and Owners' Association Disclosure Statement prior to the signing of this offer and shall have the right to terminate or withdraw this Contract without penalty (including a refund of any Due Diligence Fee) prior to WHICHEVER OF THE FOLLOWING EVENTS OCCURS FIRST: (1) the end of the third calendar day following receipt of the Disclosure Statement; (2) the end of the third calendar day following the Effective Date; or (3) Settlement or occupancy by Buyer in the case of a sale or exchange.
☐ Exempt from N.C. Residential Property and Owners' Association Disclosure Statement because (SEE GUIDELINES): _____

(e) **Mineral and Oil and Gas Rights Mandatory Disclosure Statement** *(check only one):*
☐ Buyer has received a signed copy of the N.C. Mineral and Oil and Gas Rights Mandatory Disclosure Statement prior to the signing of this offer.
☐ Buyer has NOT received a signed copy of the N.C. Mineral and Oil and Gas Rights Mandatory Disclosure Statement prior to the signing of this offer and shall have the right to terminate or withdraw this Contract without penalty (including a refund of any Due Diligence Fee) prior to WHICHEVER OF THE FOLLOWING EVENTS OCCURS FIRST: (1) the end of the third calendar day following receipt of the Disclosure Statement; (2) the end of the third calendar day following the Effective Date; or (3) Settlement or occupancy by Buyer in the case of a sale or exchange.
☐ Exempt from N.C. Mineral and Oil and Gas Rights Mandatory Disclosure Statement because (SEE GUIDELINES): _____

Buyer's receipt of a Mineral and Oil and Gas Rights Mandatory Disclosure Statement does not modify or limit the obligations of Seller under Paragraph 8(g) of this Contract and shall not constitute the assumption or approval by Buyer of any severance of mineral and/or oil and gas rights, except as may be assumed or specifically approved by Buyer in writing.

NOTE: The parties are advised to consult with a NC attorney prior to signing this Contract if severance of mineral and/or oil and gas rights has occurred or is intended.

6. **BUYER OBLIGATIONS:**
(a) **Responsibility for Proposed Special Assessments:** Buyer shall take title subject to all Proposed Special Assessments.
(b) **Responsibility for Certain Costs:** Buyer shall be responsible for all costs with respect to:
(i) any loan obtained by Buyer, including charges by an owners association and/or management company as agent of an owners' association for providing information required by Buyer's lender;

Page 6 of 14

STANDARD FORM 2-T
Revised 7/2019
© 7/2019

Buyer's initials _____   Seller's initials _____

(ii) charges required by an owners' association declaration to be paid by Buyer for Buyer's future use and enjoyment of the Property, including, without limitation, working capital contributions, membership fees, or charges for Buyer's use of the common elements and/or services provided to Buyer, such as "move-in fees";
(iii) determining restrictive covenant compliance;
(iv) appraisal;
(v) title search;
(vi) title insurance;
(vii) any fees charged by the closing attorney for the preparation of the Closing Disclosure, Seller Disclosure and any other settlement statement;
(viii) recording the deed; and
(ix) preparation and recording of all instruments required to secure the balance of the Purchase Price unpaid at Settlement.

(c) **Authorization to Disclose Information:** Buyer authorizes the Buyer's lender(s), the parties' real estate agent(s) and closing attorney: (1) to provide this Contract to any appraiser employed by Buyer or by Buyer's lender(s); and (2) to release and disclose any buyer's closing disclosure, settlement statement and/or disbursement summary, or any information therein, to the parties to this transaction, their real estate agent(s) and Buyer's lender(s).

7. **SELLER REPRESENTATIONS:**
(a) **Ownership:** Seller represents that Seller:
☐ has owned the Property for at least one year.
☐ has owned the Property for less than one year.
☐ does not yet own the Property.
(b) **Lead-Based Paint** *(check if applicable)*:
☐ The Property is residential and was built prior to 1978 (Attach Lead-Based Paint or Lead-Based Paint Hazards Disclosure Addendum {Standard Form 2A9-T}).

(c) **Assessments:** To the best of Seller's knowledge there ☐ are ☐ are not any Proposed Special Assessments. If any Proposed Special Assessments, identify: _____

Seller warrants that there ☐ are ☐ are not any Confirmed Special Assessments. If any Confirmed Special Assessments, identify:
_____

NOTE: Buyer's and Seller's respective responsibilities for Proposed and Confirmed Special Assessments are addressed in paragraphs 6(a) and 8(k).

(d) **Owners' Association(s) and Dues:** Seller authorizes and directs any owners' association, any management company of the owners' association, any insurance company and any attorney who has previously represented the Seller to release to Buyer, Buyer's agents, representative, closing attorney or lender true and accurate copies of the following items affecting the Property, including any amendments:
- Seller's statement of account
- master insurance policy showing the coverage provided and the deductible amount
- Declaration and Restrictive Covenants
- Rules and Regulations
- Articles of Incorporation
- By laws of the owners' association
- current financial statement and budget of the owners' association
- parking restrictions and information
- architectural guidelines

☐ (specify name of association): _____ whose regular assessments("dues") are $ _____ per _____. The name, address and telephone number of the president of the owners' association or the association manager is: _____

Owners' association website address, if any: _____

☐ (specify name of association): _____ whose regular assessments ("dues") are $ _____ per _____. The name, address and telephone number of the president of the owners' association or the association manager is: _____

Owners' association website address, if any: _____

Page 7 of 14

STANDARD FORM 2-T
Revised 7/2019
© 7/2019

Buyer's initials _____ Seller's initials _____

Produced with zipForm® by zipLogix 18070 Fifteen Mile Road, Fraser, Michigan 48026 www.zipLogix.com 0001

8. **SELLER OBLIGATIONS:**
   (a) **Evidence of Title, Payoff Statement(s) and Non Foreign Status:**
      (i) Seller agrees to use best efforts to provide to the closing attorney as soon as reasonably possible after the Effective Date, copies of all title information in possession of or available to Seller, including but not limited to: title insurance policies, attorney's opinions on title, surveys, covenants, deeds, notes and deeds of trust, leases, and easements relating to the Property.
      (ii) Seller shall provide to the closing attorney all information needed to obtain a written payoff statement from any lender(s) regarding any security interest in the Property as soon as reasonably possible after the Effective Date, and Seller designates the closing attorney as Seller's agent with express authority to request and obtain on Seller's behalf payoff statements and/or short-pay statements from any such lender(s).
      (iii) If Seller is not a foreign person as defined by the Foreign Investment in Real Property Tax Act, Seller shall also provide to the closing attorney a non-foreign status affidavit (pursuant to the Foreign Investment in Real Property Tax Act). In the event Seller shall not provide a non-foreign status affidavit, Seller acknowledges that there may be withholding as provided by the Internal Revenue Code.

   (b) **Authorization to Disclose Information:** Seller authorizes: (1) any attorney presently or previously representing Seller to release and disclose any title insurance policy in such attorney's file to Buyer and both Buyer's and Seller's agents and attorneys; (2) the Property's title insurer or its agent to release and disclose all materials in the Property's title insurer's (or title insurer's agent's) file to Buyer and both Buyer's and Seller's agents and attorneys and (3) the closing attorney to release and disclose any seller's closing disclosure, settlement statement and/or disbursement summary, or any information therein, to the parties to this transaction, their real estate agent(s) and Buyer's lender(s).

   (c) **Access to Property:** Seller shall provide reasonable access to the Property through the earlier of Closing or possession by Buyer, including, but not limited to, allowing Buyer and/or Buyer's agents or representatives an opportunity to (i) conduct Due Diligence, (ii)verify the satisfactory completion of negotiated repairs/improvements, and (iii) conduct a final walk-through inspection of the Property. Seller's obligation includes providing existing utilities operating at Seller's cost, including any connections and de-winterizing.

   > **NOTE:** See WARNING in paragraph 4 above for limitation on Buyer's right to terminate this Contract as a result of Buyer's continued investigation of the Property following the expiration of the Due Diligence Period.

   (d) **Removal of Seller's Property:** Seller shall remove, by the date possession is made available to Buyer, all personal property which is not a part of the purchase and all garbage and debris from the Property.

   (e) **Affidavit and Indemnification Agreement:** Seller shall furnish at Settlement an affidavit(s) and indemnification agreement(s) in form satisfactory to Buyer and Buyer's title insurer, if any, executed by Seller and any person or entity who has performed or furnished labor, services, materials or rental equipment to the Property within 120 days prior to the date of Settlement and who may be entitled to claim a lien against the Property as described in N.C.G.S. §44A-8 verifying that each such person or entity has been paid in full and agreeing to indemnify Buyer, Buyer's lender(s) and Buyer's title insurer against all loss from any cause or claim arising therefrom.

   (f) **Designation of Lien Agent, Payment and Satisfaction of Liens:** If required by N.C.G.S. §44A-11.1, Seller shall have designated a Lien Agent, and Seller shall deliver to Buyer as soon as reasonably possible a copy of the appointment of Lien Agent. All deeds of trust, deferred ad valorem taxes, liens and other charges against the Property, not assumed by Buyer, must be paid and satisfied by Seller prior to or at Settlement such that cancellation may be promptly obtained following Closing. Seller shall remain obligated to obtain any such cancellations following Closing.

   (g) **Good Title, Legal Access:** Seller shall execute and deliver a GENERAL WARRANTY DEED for the Property in recordable form no later than Settlement, which shall convey fee simple marketable and insurable title, without exception for mechanics' liens, and free of any other liens, encumbrances or defects, including those which would be revealed by a current and accurate survey of the Property, except: ad valorem taxes for the current year(prorated through the date of Settlement); utility easements and unviolated covenants, conditions or restrictions that do not materially affect the value of the Property; and such other liens, encumbrances or defects as may be assumed or specifically approved by Buyer in writing. The Property must have legal access to a public right of way.

   > **NOTE:** Buyer's failure to conduct a survey or examine title of the Property, prior to the expiration of the Due Diligence Period does not relieve the Seller of their obligation to deliver good title under this paragraph.

   > **NOTE:** If any sale of the Property may be a "short sale," consideration should be given to attaching a Short Sale Addendum Form2A14-T) as an addendum to this Contract.

Page 8 of 14

(h) **Deed, Taxes and Fees:** Seller shall pay for preparation of a deed and all other documents necessary to perform Seller's obligations under this Contract, and for state and county excise taxes, and any deferred, discounted or rollback taxes, and local conveyance fees required by law. The deed is to be made to: _____

(i) **Agreement to Pay Buyer Expenses:** Seller shall pay at Settlement $ _____ toward any of Buyer's expenses associated with the purchase of the Property, at the discretion of Buyer and/or lender, if any, including any FHA/VA lender and inspection costs that Buyer is not permitted to pay.

NOTE: Parties should review the FHA/VA Addendum prior to entering an amount in Paragraph 8(i). Certain FHA/VA lender and inspection costs CANNOT be paid by Buyer at Settlement and the amount of these should be included in the blank above.

(j) **Owners' Association Fees/Charges:** Seller shall pay: (i) any fees required for confirming Seller's account payment information on owners' association dues or assessments for payment or proration; (ii) any fees imposed by an owners' association and/or a management company as agent of the owners' association in connection with the transaction contemplated by this Contract other than those fees required to be paid by Buyer under paragraph 6(b) above; and (iii) fees incurred by Seller in completing the Residential Property and Owners' Association Disclosure Statement, and resale or other certificates related to a proposed sale of the Property.

(k) **Payment of Confirmed Special Assessments:** Seller shall pay, in full at Settlement, all Confirmed Special Assessments, whether payable in a lump sum or future installments, provided that the amount thereof can be reasonably determined or estimated. The payment of such estimated amount shall be the final payment between the Parties.

(l) **Late Listing Penalties:** All property tax late listing penalties, if any, shall be paid by Seller.

(m) **Negotiated Repairs/Improvements:** Negotiated repairs/improvements shall be made in a good and workmanlike manner and Buyer shall have the right to verify same prior to Settlement.

(n) **Seller's Failure to Comply or Breach:** If Seller fails to materially comply with any of Seller's obligations under this Paragraph 8 or Seller materially breaches this Contract, and Buyer elects to terminate this Contract as a result of such failure or breach, then the Earnest Money Deposit and the Due Diligence Fee shall be refunded to Buyer and Seller shall reimburse to Buyer the reasonable costs actually incurred by Buyer in connection with Buyer's Due Diligence without affecting any other remedies. If legal proceedings are brought by Buyer against Seller to recover the Earnest Money Deposit, the Due Diligence Fee and/or the reasonable costs actually incurred by Buyer in connection with Buyer's Due Diligence, the prevailing party in the proceeding shall be entitled to recover from the non-prevailing party reasonable attorney fees and court costs incurred in connection with the proceeding.

9. **PRORATIONS AND ADJUSTMENTS:** Unless otherwise provided, the following items shall be prorated, with Seller responsible for the prorated amounts through the date of Settlement, and either adjusted between the parties or paid at Settlement:
  (a) **Taxes on Real Property:** Ad valorem taxes and recurring governmental service fees levied with such taxes on real property shall be prorated on a calendar year basis;
  (b) **Taxes on Personal Property:** Ad valorem taxes on personal property for the entire year shall be paid by Seller unless the personal property is conveyed to Buyer, in which case, the personal property taxes shall be prorated on a calendar year basis;
  (c) **Rents:** Rents, if any, for the Property;
  (d) **Dues:** Owners' association regular assessments (dues) and other like charges.

10. **HOME WARRANTY:** Select one of the following:
  ☐ No home warranty is to be provided by Seller.
  ☐ Buyer may obtain a one-year home warranty at a cost not to exceed $ _____ which includes sales tax and Seller agrees to pay for it at Settlement.
  ☐ Seller has obtained and will provide a one-year home warranty from _____ at a cost of $ _____ which includes sales tax and will pay for it at Settlement.

NOTE: Home warranties typically have limitations on and conditions to coverage. Refer specific questions to the home warranty company.

11. **RISK OF LOSS/CONDITION OF PROPERTY AT CLOSING:** The risk of loss or damage by fire or other casualty prior to Closing shall be upon Seller. Seller is advised not to cancel existing insurance on the Property until after confirming recordation of the deed.

Page 9 of 14

STANDARD FORM 2-T
Revised 7/2019
© 7/2019

Buyer's initials _____ Seller's initials _____

Produced with zipForm® by zipLogix 18070 Fifteen Mile Road, Fraser, Michigan 48026 www.zipLogix.com 0001

Buyer's obligation to complete the transaction contemplated by this Contract shall be contingent upon the Property being in substantially the same or better condition at Closing as on the date of this offer, reasonable wear and tear excepted. If the Property is not in substantially the same or better condition at Closing as on the date of this offer, reasonable wear and tear excepted, Buyer may terminate this Contract by written notice delivered to Seller and the Earnest Money Deposit shall be refunded to Buyer. If the Property is not in such condition and Buyer does NOT elect to terminate this Contract, Buyer shall be entitled to receive, in addition to the Property, the proceeds of any insurance claim filed by Seller on account of any damage or destruction to the Property.

12. **DELAY IN SETTLEMENT/CLOSING:** Absent agreement to the contrary in this Contract or any subsequent modification thereto, if a party is unable to complete Settlement by the Settlement Date but intends to complete the transaction and is acting in good faith and with reasonable diligence to proceed to Settlement ("Delaying Party"), and if the other party is ready, willing and able to complete Settlement on the Settlement Date ("Non-Delaying Party") then the Delaying Party shall give as much notice as possible to the Non-Delaying Party and closing attorney and shall be entitled to a delay in Settlement. If the parties fail to complete Settlement and Closing within fourteen (14) days of the Settlement Date (including any amended Settlement Date agreed to in writing by the parties) or to otherwise extend the Settlement Date by written agreement, then the Delaying Party shall be in breach and the Non-Delaying Party may terminate this Contract and shall be entitled to enforce any remedies available to such party under this Contract for the breach.

13. **POSSESSION:** Possession, including all means of access to the Property (keys, codes including security codes, garage door openers, electronic devices, etc.), shall be delivered upon Closing as defined in Paragraph 1(m) unless otherwise provided below:
- [ ] A Buyer Possession Before Closing Agreement is attached (Standard Form 2A7-T)
- [ ] A Seller Possession After Closing Agreement is attached (Standard Form 2A8-T)
- [ ] Possession is subject to rights of tenant(s)

NOTE: Consider attaching Additional Provisions Addendum (Form 2A11-T) or Vacation Rental Addendum (Form 2A13-T)

14. **ADDENDA:** CHECK ALL STANDARD ADDENDA THAT MAY BE A PART OF THIS CONTRACT, IF ANY, AND ATTACH HERETO. ITEMIZE ALL OTHER ADDENDA TO THIS CONTRACT, IF ANY, AND ATTACH HERETO.

- [ ] Additional Provisions Addendum (Form 2A11-T)
- [ ] Additional Signatures Addendum (Form 3-T)
- [ ] Back-Up Contract Addendum (Form 2A1-T)
- [ ] FHA/VA Financing Addendum (Form 2A4-T)
- [ ] Lead-Based Paint Or Lead-Based Paint Hazard Addendum (Form 2A9-T)
- [ ] Loan Assumption Addendum (Form 2A6-T)
- [ ] New Construction Addendum (Form 2A3-T)
- [ ] Owners' Association Disclosure And Condominium Resale Statement Addendum (Form 2A12-T)
- [ ] Seller Financing Addendum (Form 2A5-T)
- [ ] Short Sale Addendum (Form 2A14-T)
- [ ] Vacation Rental Addendum (Form 2A13-T)

- [ ] Identify other attorney or party drafted addenda
_____
_____

NOTE: UNDER NORTH CAROLINA LAW, REAL ESTATE BROKERS ARE NOT PERMITTED TO DRAFT ADDENDA TO THIS CONTRACT.

15. **ASSIGNMENTS:** This Contract may not be assigned without the written consent of all parties except in connection with a tax-deferred exchange, but if assigned by agreement, then this Contract shall be binding on the assignee and assignee's heirs and successors.

16. **TAX-DEFERRED EXCHANGE:** In the event Buyer or Seller desires to effect a tax-deferred exchange in connection with the conveyance of the Property, Buyer and Seller agree to cooperate in effecting such exchange; provided, however, that the exchanging party shall be responsible for all additional costs associated with such exchange, and provided further, that a non-exchanging party shall not assume any additional liability with respect to such tax-deferred exchange. Buyer and Seller shall execute such additional documents, including assignment of this Contract in connection therewith, at no cost to the non-exchanging party, as shall be required to give effect to this provision.

17. **PARTIES:** This Contract shall be binding upon and shall inure to the benefit of Buyer and Seller and their respective heirs, successors and assigns. As used herein, words in the singular include the plural and the masculine includes the feminine and neuter genders, as appropriate.

18. **SURVIVAL:** If any provision herein contained which by its nature and effect is required to be observed, kept or performed after the Closing, it shall survive the Closing and remain binding upon and for the benefit of the parties hereto until fully observed, kept or performed.

Page 10 of 14

STANDARD FORM 2-T
Revised 7/2019
© 7/2019

Buyer's initials _____   Seller's initials _____

19. **ENTIRE AGREEMENT:** This Contract contains the entire agreement of the parties and there are no representations, inducements or other provisions other than those expressed herein. All changes, additions or deletions hereto must be in writing and signed by all parties. Nothing contained herein shall alter any agreement between a REALTOR® or broker and Seller or Buyer as contained in any listing agreement, buyer agency agreement, or any other agency agreement between them.

20. **CONDUCT OF TRANSACTION:** The parties agree that any action between them relating to the transaction contemplated by this Contract may be conducted by electronic means, including the signing of this Contract by one or more of them and any notice or communication given in connection with this Contract. Any written notice or communication may be transmitted to any mailing address, e-mail address or fax number set forth in the "Notice Information" section below. Any notice or communication to be given to a party herein, and any fee, deposit or other payment to be delivered to a party herein, may be given to the party or to such party's agent. Seller and Buyer agree that the "Notice Information" and "Acknowledgment of Receipt of Monies" sections below shall not constitute a material part of this Contract, and that the addition or modification of any information therein shall not constitute a rejection of an offer or the creation of a counteroffer.

21. **EXECUTION:** This Contract may be signed in multiple originals or counterparts, all of which together constitute one and the same instrument.

22. **COMPUTATION OF DAYS/TIME OF DAY:** Unless otherwise provided, for purposes of this Contract, the term "days" shall mean consecutive calendar days, including Saturdays, Sundays, and holidays, whether federal, state, local or religious. For the purposes of calculating days, the count of "days" shall begin on the day following the day upon which any act or notice as provided in this Contract was required to be performed or made. Any reference to a date or time of day shall refer to the date and/or time of day in the State of North Carolina.

[THIS SPACE INTENTIONALLY LEFT BLANK]

Page 11 of 14

STANDARD FORM 2-T
Revised 7/2019
© 7/2019

Buyer's initials _____ Seller's initials _____

Produced with zipForm® by zipLogix 18070 Fifteen Mile Road, Fraser, Michigan 48026 www.zipLogix.com   0001

THE NORTH CAROLINA ASSOCIATION OF REALTORS®, INC. AND THE NORTH CAROLINA BAR ASSOCIATION MAKE NO REPRESENTATION AS TO THE LEGAL VALIDITY OR ADEQUACY OF ANY PROVISION OF THIS FORM IN ANY SPECIFIC TRANSACTION. IF YOU DO NOT UNDERSTAND THIS FORM OR FEEL THAT IT DOES NOT PROVIDE FOR YOUR LEGAL NEEDS, YOU SHOULD CONSULT A NORTH CAROLINA REAL ESTATE ATTORNEY BEFORE YOU SIGN IT.

This offer shall become a binding contract on the Effective Date. Unless specifically provided otherwise, Buyer's failure to timely deliver any fee, deposit or other payment provided for herein shall not prevent this offer from becoming a binding contract, provided that any such failure shall give Seller certain rights to terminate the contract as described herein or as otherwise permitted by law.

Date: _____   Date: _____

Buyer _____   Seller _____

Date: _____   Date: _____

Buyer _____   Seller _____

Entity Buyer: Entity Seller:
_____   _____
   (Name of LLC/Corporation/Partnership/Trust/etc.)   (Name of LLC/Corporation/Partnership/Trust/etc.)
By: _____   By: _____

Name: _____   Name: _____
      Print Name   Print Name
Title: _____   Title: _____

Date: _____   Date: _____

WIRE FRAUD WARNING

TO BUYERS: BEFORE SENDING ANY WIRE, YOU SHOULD CALL THE CLOSING ATTORNEY'S OFFICE TO VERIFY THE INSTRUCTIONS. IF YOU RECEIVE WIRING INSTRUCTIONS FOR A DIFFERENT BANK, BRANCH LOCATION, ACCOUNT NAME OR ACCOUNT NUMBER, THEY SHOULD BE PRESUMED FRAUDULENT. DO NOT SEND ANY FUNDS AND CONTACT THE CLOSING ATTORNEY'S OFFICE IMMEDIATELY.

TO SELLERS: IF YOUR PROCEEDS WILL BE WIRED, IT IS RECOMMENDED THAT YOU PROVIDE WIRING INSTRUCTIONS AT CLOSING IN WRITING IN THE PRESENCE OF THE ATTORNEY. IF YOU ARE UNABLE TO ATTEND CLOSING, YOU MAY BE REQUIRED TO SEND AN ORIGINAL NOTARIZED DIRECTIVE TO THE CLOSING ATTORNEY'S OFFICE CONTAINING THE WIRING INSTRUCTIONS. THIS MAY BE SENT WITH THE DEED, LIEN WAIVER AND TAX FORMS IF THOSE DOCUMENTS ARE BEING PREPARED FOR YOU BY THE CLOSING ATTORNEY. AT A MINIMUM, YOU SHOULD CALL THE CLOSING ATTORNEY'S OFFICE TO PROVIDE THE WIRE INSTRUCTIONS. THE WIRE INSTRUCTIONS SHOULD BE VERIFIED OVER THE TELEPHONE VIA A CALL TO YOU INITIATED BY THE CLOSING ATTORNEY'S OFFICE TO ENSURE THAT THEY ARE NOT FROM A FRAUDULENT SOURCE.

WHETHER YOU ARE A BUYER OR A SELLER, YOU SHOULD CALL THE CLOSING ATTORNEY'S OFFICE AT A NUMBER THAT IS INDEPENDENTLY OBTAINED. TO ENSURE THAT YOUR CONTACT IS LEGITIMATE, YOU SHOULD NOT RELY ON A PHONE NUMBER IN AN EMAIL FROM THE CLOSING ATTORNEY'S OFFICE, YOUR REAL ESTATE AGENT OR ANYONE ELSE.

STANDARD FORM 2-T
Revised 7/2019
© 7/2019

Produced with zipForm® by zipLogix 18070 Fifteen Mile Road, Fraser, Michigan 48026   www.zipLogix.com   0001

NOTICE INFORMATION

NOTE: INSERT AT LEAST ONE ADDRESS AND/OR ELECTRONIC DELIVERY ADDRESS EACH PARTY AND AGENT APPROVES FOR THE RECEIPT OF ANY NOTICE CONTEMPLATED BY THIS CONTRACT. INSERT "N/A" FOR ANY WHICH ARE NOT APPROVED.

BUYER NOTICE ADDRESS:

Mailing Address: _____

_____

Buyer Fax#: _____

Buyer E-mail: _____

SELLER NOTICE ADDRESS:

Mailing Address: _____

_____

Seller Fax#: _____

Seller E-mail: _____

CONFIRMATION OF AGENCY/NOTICE ADDRESSES

Selling Firm Name: _____
Acting as ☐ Buyer's Agent ☐ Seller's(sub)Agent ☐ Dual Agent
Firm License #: _____
Mailing Address: _____

_____

Individual Selling Agent: _____
☐ Acting as a Designated Dual Agent (check only if applicable)

Selling Agent License #: _____

Selling Agent Phone#: _____

Selling Agent Fax#: _____

Selling Agent E-mail: _____

Listing Firm Name: _____
Acting as ☐ Seller's Agent ☐ Dual Agent
Firm License #: _____
Mailing Address: _____

_____

Individual Listing Agent: **R. Allen Lyles** _____
☐ Acting as a Designated Dual Agent (check only if applicable)

Listing Agent License #: _____

Listing Agent Phone#: **(919)932-9623**

Listing Agent Fax#: _____

Listing Agent E-mail: **allen.lyles@DMPropNC.com**

[THIS SPACE INTENTIONALLY LEFT BLANK]

STANDARD FORM 2-T
Revised 7/2019
© 7/2019

Buyer's initials _____   Seller's initials _____

Produced with zipForm® by zipLogix 18070 Fifteen Mile Road, Fraser, Michigan 48026   www.zipLogix.com   0001

ACKNOWLEDGMENT OF RECEIPT OF MONIES

Seller: _____ ("Seller")

Buyer: _____ ("Buyer")

Property Address: _____ ("Property")

☐ **LISTING AGENT ACKNOWLEDGMENT OF RECEIPT OF DUE DILIGENCE FEE**

Paragraph 1(d) of the Offer to Purchase and Contract between Buyer and Seller for the sale of the Property provides for the payment to Seller of a Due Diligence Fee in the amount of $ _____ , receipt of which Listing Agent hereby acknowledges.

Date: _____   Firm: _____

                                         By: _____
                                                        (Signature)
                                                   R. Allen Lyles
                                                    (Print name)

☐ **SELLER ACKNOWLEDGMENT OF RECEIPT OF DUE DILIGENCE FEE**

Paragraph 1(d) of the Offer to Purchase and Contract between Buyer and Seller for the sale of the Property provides for the payment to Seller of a Due Diligence Fee in the amount of $ _____ , receipt of which Seller hereby acknowledges.

Date: _____   Seller: _____
                                                        (Signature)

Date: _____   Seller: _____
                                                        (Signature)

☐ **ESCROW AGENT ACKNOWLEDGMENT OF RECEIPT OF INITIAL EARNEST MONEY DEPOSIT**

Paragraph 1(d) of the Offer to Purchase and Contract between Buyer and Seller for the sale of the Property provides for the payment to Escrow Agent of an Initial Earnest Money Deposit in the amount of $ _____ . Escrow Agent as identified in Paragraph 1(f) of the Offer to Purchase and Contract hereby acknowledges receipt of the Initial Earnest Money Deposit and agrees to hold and disburse the same in accordance with the terms of the Offer to Purchase and Contract.

Date: _____   Firm: _____

                                         By: _____
                                                        (Signature)

                                         _____
                                                        (Print name)

☐ **ESCROW AGENT ACKNOWLEDGMENT OF RECEIPT OF (ADDITIONAL) EARNEST MONEY DEPOSIT**

Paragraph 1(d) of the Offer to Purchase and Contract between Buyer and Seller for the sale of the Property provides for the payment to Escrow Agent of an (Additional) Earnest Money Deposit in the amount of $ _____ . Escrow Agent as identified in Paragraph 1(f) of the Offer to Purchase and Contract hereby acknowledges receipt of the (Additional) Earnest Money Deposit and agrees to hold and disburse the same in accordance with the terms of the Offer to Purchase and Contract.

Date: _____   Firm: _____

Time: _____ ☐ A.M. ☐ P.M.   By: _____
                                                        (Signature)

                                         _____
                                                        (Print name)

Page 14 of 14

STANDARD FORM 2-T
Revised 7/2019
© 7/2019

SAMPLE PROMISSORY NOTE

PROMISSORY NOTE

SATISFACTION: The debt evidenced by
this Note has been satisfied in full this
_____ day of _____ , _____
Signed: _____

_____ , N.C.

$ _____   Date _____

FOR VALUE RECEIVED the undersigned, jointly and severally, promise to pay to _____
_____ or order,

the principal sum of _____
DOLLARS ($ _____), with interest from _____ . at the rate of _____
per cent (_____%) per annum on the unpaid balance until paid or until default, both principal and interest payable in lawful money of the United
States of America, at the office of _____

or at such place as the legal holder hereof may designate in writing. It is understood and agreed that additional amounts may be advanced by the
holder hereof as provided in the instruments, if any, securing this Note and such advances will be added to the principal of this Note and will accrue
interest at the above specified rate of interest from the date of advance until paid. The principal and interest shall be due and payable as follows:

If not sooner paid, the entire remaining indebtedness shall be due and payable on _____ .

If payable in installments, each such installment shall, unless otherwise provided, be applied first to payment of interest then accrued and due on the
unpaid principal balance, with the remainder applied to the unpaid principal.

Unless otherwise provided, this Note may be prepaid in full or in part at any time without penalty or premium. Partial prepayments shall be applied
to installments due in reverse order of their maturity.

In the event of (a) default in payment of any installment of principal or interest hereof as the same becomes due and such default is not cured within ten
(10) days from the due date, or (b) default under the terms of any instrument securing this Note, and such default is not cured within fifteen (15) days
after written notice to maker, then in either such event the holder may without further notice, declare the remainder of the principal sum, together with
all interest accrued thereon and, the prepayment premium, if any, at once due and payable. Failure to exercise this option shall not constitute a
waiver of the right to exercise the same at any other time. The unpaid principal of this Note and any part thereof, accrued interest and all other sums
due under this Note and the Deed of Trust, if any, shall bear interest at the rate of _____
per cent (_____%) per annum after default until paid.

All parties to this Note, including maker and any sureties, endorsers, or guarantors hereby waive protest, presentment, notice of dishonor, and notice of acceleration of maturity and agree to continue to remain bound for the payment of principal, interest and all other sums due under this Note and Deed of Trust notwithstanding any change or changes by way of release, surrender, exchange, modification or substitution of any security for this Note or by way of any extension or extensions of time for the payment of principal and interest; and all such parties waive all and every kind of notice of such change or changes and agree that the same may be made without notice or consent of any of them.

Upon default the holder of this Note may employ an attorney to enforce the holder's rights and remedies and the maker, principal, surety, guarantor and endorsers of this Note hereby agree to pay to the holder reasonable attorneys fees not exceeding a sum equal to fifteen percent (15%) of the outstanding balance owing on said Note, plus all other reasonable expenses incurred by the holder in exercising any of the holder's rights and remedies upon default. The rights and remedies of the holder as provided in this Note and any instrument securing this Note shall be cumulative and may be pursued singly, successively, or together against the property described in the Deed of Trust or any other funds, property or security held by the holder for payment or security, in the sole discretion of the holder. The failure to exercise any such right or remedy shall not be a waiver or release of such rights or remedies or the right to exercise any of them at another time.

This Note is to be governed and construed in accordance with the laws of the State of North Carolina.

This Note is given _____ and is secured by a

_____ which is a _____ lien upon the property therein described.

IN TESTIMONY WHEREOF, each corporate maker has caused this instrument to be executed in its corporate name by its _____ President, attested by its _____ Secretary, and its corporate seal to be hereto affixed, all by order of its Board of Directors first duly given, the day and year first above written.

(Corporate Name)
By: _____
_____ President
ATTEST:

_____ Secretary (Corporate Seal)

(Corporate Name)
By: _____
_____ President
ATTEST:

_____ Secretary (Corporate Seal)

IN TESTIMONY WHEREOF, each individual maker has hereunto set his hand and adopted as his seal the word "SEAL" appearing beside his name, the day and year first above written.

_____ (SEAL)

_____ (SEAL)

_____ (SEAL)

_____ (SEAL)

_____ (SEAL)

_____ (SEAL)

_____ (SEAL)

SAMPLE DEED OF TRUST (MORTGAGE)

NORTH CAROLINA DEED OF TRUST

SATISFACTION: The debt secured by the within Deed of Trust together with the note(s) secured thereby has been satisfied in full.

This the _____ day of _____ , 20 _____

Signed: _____   _____

_____   _____

Parcel Identifier No. _____ Verified by _____ County on the _____ day of _____ , 20 _____
By: _____

Mail/Box to: _____
This instrument was prepared by: _____
Brief Description for the index: _____

THIS DEED of TRUST made this _____ day of _____ , 20 _____ , by and between:

GRANTOR	TRUSTEE	BENEFICIARY

Enter in appropriate block for each party: name, address, and, if appropriate, character of entity, e.g. corporation or partnership.

THIS DEED OF TRUST SECURES 1 PROMISSORY NOTE OF EVEN DATE HEREWITH IN THE AMOUNT OF $40,000.00

The designation Grantor, Trustee, and Beneficiary as used herein shall include said parties, their heirs, successors, and assigns, and shall include singular, plural, masculine, feminine or neuter as required by context.

WITNESSETH, That whereas the Grantor is indebted to the Beneficiary in the principal sum of _____
_____ Dollars ($ _____),
as evidenced by a Promissory Note of even date herewith, the terms of which are incorporated herein by reference. The final due date for payments of said Promissory Note, if not sooner paid, is _____ , 20 _____ .

NOW, THEREFORE, as security for said indebtedness, advancements and other sums expended by Beneficiary pursuant to this Deed of Trust and costs of collection (including attorneys fees as provided in the Promissory Note) and other valuable consideration, the receipt of which is hereby acknowledged, the Grantor has bargained, sold, given and conveyed and does by these presents bargain, sell, give, grant and convey to said Trustee, his heirs, or successors, and assigns, the parcel(s) of land situated in the City of _____ _____ County, North Carolina, (the "Premises") and more particularly described as follows:

SEE EXHIBIT "A"

TO HAVE AND TO HOLD said Premises with all privileges and appurtenances thereunto belonging, to said Trustee, his heirs, successors, and assigns forever, upon the trusts, terms and conditions, and for the uses hereinafter set forth.

If the Grantor shall pay the Note secured hereby in accordance with its terms, together with interest thereon, and any renewals or extensions thereof in whole or in part, all other sums secured hereby shall comply with all of the covenants, terms and conditions of this Deed of Trust, then this conveyance shall be null and void and may be cancelled of record at the request and the expense of the Grantor.

If, however, there shall be any default (a) in the payment of any sums due under the Note, this Deed of Trust or any other instrument securing the Note and such default is not cured within ten (10) days from the due date, or (b) if there shall be default in any of the other covenants, terms or conditions of the Note secured hereby, or any failure or neglect to comply with the covenants, terms or conditions contained in this Deed of Trust or any other instrument securing the Note and such default is not cured within fifteen (15) days after written notice, then and in any of such events, without further notice, it shall be lawful for and the duty of the Trustee, upon request of the Beneficiary, to sell the land herein conveyed at public auction for cash, after having first giving such notice of hearing as to commencement of foreclosure proceedings and obtained such findings or leave of court as may then be required by law and giving such notice and advertising the time and place of such sale in such manner as may then be provided by law, and upon such and any resales and upon compliance with the law then relating to foreclosure proceedings under power of sale to convey title to the purchaser in as full and ample manner as the Trustee is empowered. The Trustee shall be authorized to retain an attorney to represent him in such proceedings.

The proceeds of the Sale shall after the Trustee retains his commission, together with reasonable attorneys fees incurred by the Trustee in such proceedings, be applied to the costs of sale, including, but not limited to, costs of collection, taxes, assessments, costs of recording, service fees and incidental expenditures, the amount due on the Note hereby secured and advancements and other sums expended by the Beneficiary according to the provisions hereof and otherwise as required by the then existing law relating to foreclosures. The Trustee's commission shall be five percent (5%) of the gross proceeds of the sale or the minimum sum of $ 500.00 whichever is greater, for a completed foreclosure. In the event foreclosure is commenced, but not completed, the Grantor shall pay all expenses incurred by Trustee including reasonable attorneys fees, and a partial commission computed on five per cent (5%) of the outstanding indebtedness or the above stated minimum sum, whichever is greater, in accordance with the following schedule, to-wit: one-fourth (1/4) thereof before the Trustee issues a notice of hearing on the right to foreclosure; one-half (1/2) thereof after issuance of said notice; three-fourths (3/4) thereof after such hearing, and the greater of the full commission or minimum sum after the initial sale.

And the said Grantor does hereby covenant and agree with the Trustee as follows:

1. INSURANCE. Grantor shall keep all improvements on said land, now or hereafter erected, constantly insured for the benefit of the Beneficiary against loss by fire, windstorm and such other casualties and contingencies, in such manner and in such companies and for such amounts, not less than that amount necessary to pay the sum secured by this Deed of Trust, and as may be satisfactory to the Beneficiary. Grantor shall purchase such insurance, pay all premiums therefor, and shall deliver to Beneficiary such policies along with evidence of premium payment as long as the Note secured hereby remains unpaid. If Grantor fails to purchase such insurance, pay premiums therefor or deliver said policies along with evidence of payment of premiums thereon, then Beneficiary, at his option, may purchase such insurance. Such amounts paid by Beneficiary shall be added to the principal of the Note secured by this Deed of Trust, and shall be due and payable upon demand of Beneficiary. All proceeds from any insurance so maintained shall at the option of Beneficiary be applied to the debt secured hereby and if payable in installments, applied in the inverse order of maturity of such installments or to the repair or reconstruction of any improvements located upon the Property.

2. TAXES, ASSESSMENTS, CHARGES. Grantor shall pay all taxes, assessments and charges as may be lawfully levied against said Premises within thirty (30) days after the same shall become due. In the event that Grantor fails to so pay all taxes, assessments and charges as herein required, then Beneficiary, at his option, may pay the same and the amounts so paid shall be added to the principal of the Note secured by this Deed of Trust, and shall be due and payable upon demand of Beneficiary.

3. ASSIGNMENTS OF RENTS AND PROFITS. Grantor assigns to Beneficiary, in the event of default, all rents and profits from the land and any improvements thereon, and authorizes Beneficiary to enter upon and take possession of such land and improvements, to rent same, at any reasonable rate of rent determined by Beneficiary, and after deducting from any such rents the cost of reletting and collection, to apply the remainder to the debt secured hereby.

4. PARTIAL RELEASE. Grantor shall not be entitled to the partial release of any of the above described property unless a specific provision providing therefor is included in this Deed of Trust. In the event a partial release provision is included in this Deed of Trust, Grantor must strictly comply with the terms thereof. Notwithstanding anything herein contained, Grantor shall not be entitled to any release of property unless Grantor is not in default and is in full compliance with all of the terms and provisions of the Note, this Deed of Trust, and any other instrument that may be securing said Note.

5. WASTE. The Grantor covenants that he will keep the Premises herein conveyed in as good order, repair and condition as they are now, reasonable wear and tear excepted, and will comply with all governmental requirements respecting the Premises or their use, and that he will not commit or permit any waste.

6. CONDEMNATION. In the event that any or all of the Premises shall be condemned and taken under the power of eminent domain, Grantor shall give immediate written notice to Beneficiary and Beneficiary shall have the right to receive and collect all damages awarded by reason of such taking, and the right to such damages hereby is assigned to Beneficiary who shall have the discretion to apply the amount so received, or any part thereof, to

the indebtedness due hereunder and if payable in installments, applied in the inverse order of maturity of such installments, or to any alteration, repair or restoration of the Premises by Grantor.

7. WARRANTIES. Grantor covenants with Trustee and Beneficiary that he is seized of the Premises in fee simple, has the right to convey the same in fee simple, that title is marketable and free and clear of all encumbrances, and that he will warrant and defend the title against the lawful claims of all persons whomsoever, except for the exceptions hereinabove stated. Title to the property hereinafter described is subject to the following exceptions:

8. SUBSTITUTION OF TRUSTEE. Grantor and Trustee covenant and agree to and with Beneficiary that in case the said Trustee, or any successor trustee, shall die, become incapable of acting, renounce his trust, or for any reason the holder of the Note desires to replace said Trustee, then the holder may appoint, in writing, a trustee to take the place of the Trustee; and upon the probate and registration of the same, the trustee thus appointed shall succeed to all rights, powers and duties of the Trustee.

THE FOLLOWING PARAGRAPH, 9. SALE OF PREMISES, SHALL NOT APPLY UNLESS THE BLOCK TO THE LEFT MARGIN OF THIS SENTENCE IS MARKED AND/OR INITIALED.

9. SALE OF PREMISES. Grantor agrees that if the Premises or any part thereof or interest therein is sold, assigned, transferred, conveyed or otherwise alienated by Grantor, whether voluntarily or involuntarily or by operation of law [other than: (i) the creation of a lien or other encumbrance subordinate to this Deed of Trust which does not relate to a transfer of rights of occupancy in the Premises; (ii) the creation of a purchase money security interest for household appliances; (iii) a transfer by devise, descent, or operation of law on the death of a joint tenant or tenant by the entirety; (iv) the grant of a leasehold interest of three (3) years or less not containing an option to purchase; (v) a transfer to relative resulting from the death of a Grantor; (vi) a transfer where the spouse or children of the Grantor become the owner of the Premises; (vii) a transfer resulting from a decree of a dissolution of marriage, legal separation agreement, or from an incidental property settlement agreement, by which the spouse of the Grantor becomes an owner of the Premises; (viii) a transfer into an inter vivos trust in which the Grantor is and remains a beneficiary and which does not relate to a transfer of rights of occupancy in the Premises], without the prior written consent of Beneficiary, Beneficiary, at its own option, may declare the Note secured hereby and all other obligations hereunder to be forthwith due and payable. Any change in the legal or equitable title of the Premises or in the beneficial ownership of the Premises, including the sale, conveyance or disposition of a majority interest in the Grantor if a corporation or partnership, whether or not of record and whether or not for consideration, shall be deemed to be the transfer of an interest in the Premises.

10. ADVANCEMENTS. If Grantor shall fail to perform any of the covenants or obligations contained herein or in any other instrument given as additional security for the Note secured hereby, the Beneficiary may, but without obligation, make advances to perform such covenants or obligations, and all such sums so advanced shall be added to the principal sum, shall bear interest at the rate provided in the Note secured hereby for sums due after default and shall be due from Grantor on demand of the Beneficiary. No advancement or anything contained in this paragraph shall constitute a waiver by Beneficiary or prevent such failure to perform from constituting an event of default.

11. INDEMNITY. If any suit or proceeding be brought against the Trustee or Beneficiary or if any suit or proceeding be brought which may affect the value or title of the Premises, Grantor shall defend, indemnify and hold harmless and on demand reimburse Trustee or Beneficiary from any loss, cost, damage or expense and any sums expended by Trustee or Beneficiary shall bear interest as provided in the Note secured hereby for sums due after default and shall be due and payable on demand.

12. WAIVERS. Grantor waives all rights to require marshalling of assets by the Trustee or Beneficiary. No delay or omission of the Trustee or Beneficiary in the exercise of any right, power or remedy arising under the Note or this Deed of Trust shall be deemed a waiver of any default or acquiescence therein or shall impair or waive the exercise of such right, power or remedy by Trustee or Beneficiary at any other time.

13. CIVIL ACTION. In the event that the Trustee is named as a party to any civil action as Trustee in this Deed of Trust, the Trustee shall be entitled to employ an attorney at law, including himself if he is a licensed attorney, to represent him in said action and the reasonable attorney's fee of the Trustee in such action shall be paid by the Beneficiary and added to the principal of the Note secured by this Deed of Trust and bear interest at the rate provided in the Note for sums due after default.

14. PRIOR LIENS. Default under the terms of any instrument secured by a lien to which this Deed of Trust is subordinate shall constitute default hereunder.

15. OTHER TERMS.

IN WITNESS WHEREOF, the Grantor has duly executed the foregoing as of the day and year first above written.

_____   _____ (SEAL)

By: _____   _____ (SEAL)

    Title: _____

By: _____   _____ (SEAL)

    Title: _____

By: _____   _____ (SEAL)

    Title: _____

                                     _____ (SEAL)

                                       _____ (SEAL)

                                       _____ (SEAL)

SEAL - STAMP   *USE BLACK INK ONLY*

State of North Carolina - County of _____

I, the undersigned Notary Public of the County and State aforesaid, certify that _____

_____ personally appeared before me this day and acknowledged the due execution of the foregoing instrument for the purposes therein expressed. Witness my hand and Notorial stamp or seal, this _____ day of _____ , 20 _____.

My Commission expires: _____   _____

                                                    Notary Public

---

SEAL - STAMP   *USE BLACK INK ONLY*

State of North Carolina - County of _____

I, the undersigned Notary Public of the County and State aforesaid, certify that _____

_____ personally came before me this day and acknowledged that he is the _____ of _____, a North Carolina or _____ Corporation and that by authority duly given and as the act of each entity, he signed the foregoing instrument in its name on its behalf as its act and deed. Witness my hand and Notarial stamp or seal this _____ day of _____ , 2020.

My Commission expires: _____   _____

                                                    Notary Public

---

SEAL - STAMP

Use Black Ink   *USE BLACK INK ONLY*

State of North Carolina - County of _____

I, the undersigned Notary Public of the County and State aforesaid, certify that _____

_____ personally appeared before me this day and acknowledged the due execution of the foregoing instrument for the purposes therein expressed. Witness my hand and Notorial stamp or seal, this _____ day of _____ , 20 _____.

My Commission expires: _____   _____

                                                    Notary Public

---

The foregoing Certificate(s) of _____ is/are certified to be correct.

This instrument and this certificate are duly registered at the date and time and in the Book and Page shown on the first page hereof.

_____ Register of Deeds for _____ County

By: _____ Deputy/Assistant - Register of Deeds.

SELF-DIRECTED IRA DIRECTION OF INVESTMENT LETTER

PROMISSORY NOTE PROCEDURES

QUEST TRUST COMPANY

PLEASE USE THIS GUIDE WHEN INVESTING IN PROMISSORY NOTES THROUGH YOUR IRA

Review and complete all the documents in this packet, and return to Quest Trust Company. *Typical processing time is 24-48 hours from once all executed documents and completed investment forms are received and reviewed.*

One of the following documents must be submitted along with the Direction of Investment Form for Promissory Notes.

Items Needed for Funding Notes Secured by Real Estate:

☐ New Note: Submit a copy of the drafted Promissory Note and Deed of Trust/Mortgage.

☐ Existing Note: Submit a copy of the existing Promissory Note, Deed of Trust/Mortgage, and a copy of all Transfer Liens.*

Please note that fully executed documents must be provided to QTC within 30 days of funding.

Items Needed for Funding Notes Secured by Collateral (Non-Real Estate)

☐ New Note: Submit the Original Promissory Note with the borrower's wet ink signature, and the Original Security Agreement with the borrower's wet ink signature.

☐ Existing Note: Submit a copy of the Existing Promissory Note, Existing Security Agreement, and Allonge.

Items Needed for Funding Unsecured Notes:

☐ New Note: Submit the Original Promissory Note with the borrower's wet ink signature.

☐ Existing Note: Submit a copy of the Existing Promissory Note and Allonge.

NOTE: Quest Trust Company is the legal entity in administration of the IRA and thus must sign as the lender. We CANNOT sign anything without the client's written approval. Client must sign "Read & Approved" on each page that requires a signature or initial from Quest Trust.

Normal processing for investments will be completed within 24-48 hours unless amendments are required. If completed paperwork and documentation is received before 10:30 AM central time, the processing period begins on current business day. If the documentation requires any amendments, this could delay review until all documents are completed.

⚠ All transactions done in an IRA must be on an arms length basis and for investment purposes only.

⚠ It is up to the client to determine if the interest rate on your promissory note complies with the applicable state laws, such as usury laws in Texas.

THINGS TO REMEMBER

1. Please ensure your Quest Trust Self-Directed IRA has been established and funds have cleared.

2. The first step in funding this transaction is to make sure the vesting for the lender is as follows:
   • Quest Trust Company FBO (account holders name) IRA # (account number)

3. Quest Trust CANNOT sign any of the documents without the client completing their "Read & Approved" signature.

4. The lender's address should be the Quest Trust Houston Corporate Office address.
   • 17171 Park Row, Suite 100 Houston, TX 77084

DISCLAIMER: Quest Trust Company does not sell or endorse any investment products, and are not affiliated in any way with any investment provider. Quest Trust Company does not assume responsibility for any tax, legal or investment advise with respect to this investment and is not liable for any loss which results from this investment. Quest Trust Company will not review the merits, legitimacy, appropriateness or suitability of this investments and all clients must do their own due diligence.

DOCUMENTS COMPLETED?

Secured Document Upload

- Submit your documents electronically though the secured document upload. UPLOAD.QUESTTRUSTCOMPANY.COM
- Corporate – 17171 Park Row, Ste 100, Houston, TX 77084
- Fax- 281.646.9701

If you are unsure of what form to use or how to complete a form, help is only an email or phone call away!

WWW.QUESTTRUSTCOMPANY.COM | 855.FUN.IRAS (855.386.4727)

Direction of Investment
Promissory Notes

Quest Trust Company
17171 Park Row, Suite 100
Houston, TX 77084
P: 800.320.5950
F: 281.646.9701
Documents@QuestTrust.com

QUEST TRUST
C O M P A N Y

Processing Instructions: The official processing of investment documents begins on the first business day in which all investment forms and correctly vested agreements are properly endorsed and submitted to Quest Trust Company. Once all forms and agreements have been correctly submitted, funding can be expected within 48 business hours of that time.
Use this form to direct Quest Trust Company to fund an investment for your account. All investment documents must be titled in the following format:
Quest Trust Company FBO [Account Holder's Name] [IRA or HSA or CESA] #[Account Number]

A. ACCOUNT HOLDER INFORMATION

Legal Name: Account Number:

Account Type:
○ Traditional IRA   ○ Roth IRA   ○ SEP IRA   ○ SIMPLE IRA   ○ HSA   ○ ESA

B. HOW WOULD YOU LIKE TO PAY YOUR FEES?   (ALL FEES ARE DUE PRIOR TO FUNDING)

Fees Due:
$125.00 Transaction Fee $35.00 Overnight Mail (If applicable)
$30.00 Wire Transfer (If applicable) $5.00 ACH Transfer (If applicable)
$295.00 Administrative Fee (If applicable)

Choose A Payment Method:
○ Deduct From Account   ○ Check Enclosed   ○ Credit Card on File
To add, change, or update a credit card, please contact our office.

C. INVESTMENT DETAILS

Note Type:
○ New Note   ○ Additional Funding to Existing Note   ○ Purchase of Existing Note   ○ Seller Financed Note*   ○ Convertible Note
*Please also submit a Direction to Sell for Real Estate OR use an Asset Conversion Form.

Principal Amount of Note: Dollar Amount to be Funded: Interest Rate: Maturity Date:

Percentage of Ownership in Account: Type of Payment: ○ Interest Only   ○ Amortized*
If this investment is split amongst other Quest account holders, please note that   ○ Other:_____
all incoming payments for this investment will be split according to the
percentage of ownership indicated above, UNLESS prior written authorization   *If amortized, please include copy of amortization schedule.
has been given by all Quest account holders privy to this investment.   Payment Amount:_____

Borrower's Name (Individual or Entity Name):   If borrower is entity, please provide name of Managing Member:

Borrower's Street Address: Borrower's City, State, Zip Code:

D. LOAN COLLATERAL

○ **Unsecured (Please read and initial below)**

    I acknowledge that Quest Trust Company did not recommend this investment nor are they responsible to perform any due diligence on this investment.
——   I acknowledge that this loan is unsecured and is not guaranteed by Quest Trust Company or any other party, entity or individual.

○ **Secured (Please read and initial below)**

    I understand that Quest Trust Company will not record any collateral documents, including, but not limited to mortgages, deeds of trust, or other liens,
——   with any county or governing body. I understand it is my responsibility to ensure proper recording is done regardless of whether funds are sent through
    a title company or directly to the borrower.
    Loan Secured by:
    ○ Real Estate: Property Address:_____
        Title Company Name and Contact:_____
    ○ Mobile Home: VIN:_____
    ○ Other: Description:_____

Page 1 of 3
Quest Trust Company, Rev. 01/2020

Direction of Investment — Promissory Notes

Quest Trust Company
17171 Park Row, Suite 100
Houston, TX 77084
P: 800.320.5950
F: 281.646.9701
Documents@QuestTrust.com

E. EXECUTED DOCUMENTS ACKNOWLEDGEMENT

Quest Trust Company requires fully executed documents to hold any asset in your account. Fully executed documents are documents that have been signed by all parties (lender and borrower). The reason we require these documents is because they prove, legally, that your IRA owns the aforementioned investment. If we do not receive these documents within 30 days of funding your investment, we may, at any time, distribute the asset out of your IRA and back to you, personally, at full face value. Note: Typically, if you are closing at a title company or with a fee attorney, these executed documents will be forwarded to our office after closing has occurred.

I acknowledge and ensure that QTC will receive fully executed documents within 30 days of the funding of this investment. I agree and understand that failure to submit these documents may lead to distribution of the asset at full face value.

F. FAIR MARKET VALUATIONS

Updated Annual Valuation: The Internal Revenue Service (IRS) requires that the value of all assets in my account must be updated annually at the end of each calendar year, including this asset I intend to purchase. To satisfy this requirement, please review the following options available to you:

○ I will obtain an independent qualified valuation and provide it to Quest Trust Company when requested. *

○ I authorize Quest Trust Company to obtain a qualified valuation as outlined above. I understand and agree that the charge for this service will be the cost of the valuation plus $50. **

*By making this election, I agree to provide the prior year-end value of this investment by no later than January 15th of each year on a form provided by the Custodian, with substantiation attached to support the value provided.

**Please note that QTC will, to the best of our abilities, attempt to obtain the annual valuation for this asset by utilizing the information you have provided on this form. However, if QTC is unable to collect the information, we will notify you and a fee will not be assessed. In addition, this authorization only covers annual fair market valuations. You are responsible for providing the valuation related to any taxable events (e.g. in-kind distribution or Roth conversion).

G. THIRD PARTY SERVICER

The loan servicer is who will monitor payments made to the account. Quest Trust Company receives payments and record-keeps but does not service loans or monitor the timeliness of payments made.

Servicer: ○ Account Holder ○ Third Party

Loan Servicer Name: ____ | Point of Contact: ____

Phone Number: ____ | Email Address: ____

H. FUNDING INSTRUCTIONS

Process this investment via ○ Wire ($30 Fee) ○ ACH ($5 Fee) ○ Check ($5 Fee)

FOR ACH/WIRE		FOR CHECK
Name of Bank:	Account Name:	Make Check Payable to:
ABA/Routing Number:	Account Number:	Mail Check to:
For Further Credit to:		Send Check via: ○ Regular Mail ○ Overnight Mail ($35) ○ Hold for pickup ○ Houston office ○ Austin office ○ Dallas office

I. DISQUALIFIED PERSONS (PARTIES IN INTEREST) STATEMENT

Please answer the following questions as it relates to these individuals: **you, your spouse, your children or other direct descendants or their spouses, or your parents or other direct ascendants.**

1. Are any of the above mentioned individuals, either personally or through an entity, a borrower or borrowing entity on this note?
○ Yes ○ No

2. Will any of the above mentioned individuals or any other disqualified person receive a personal gain or benefit as a result of the purchase of this note?
○ Yes ○ No
If yes to any of the questions above, please explain: ____

QUEST TRUST
COMPANY

Direction of Investment
Promissory Notes

Quest Trust Company
17171 Park Row, Suite 100
Houston, TX 77084
P: 800.320.5950
F: 281.646.9701
Documents@QuestTrust.com

I. AUTHORIZATION

I confirm that I am directing Quest Trust Company (QTC), as Custodian of my account, to complete this transaction as specified above. I specifically authorize the Custodian to execute any and all documents necessary to complete this transaction. I understand that my account is self-directed, and I take complete responsibility for any investment I choose for my account, including the investment specified in this Direction of Investment. I understand that the Custodian does not sell or endorse any investment products, and that they are not affiliated in any way with any investment provider. I understand that the role of the Custodian is limited, and the Custodian's responsibilities do not include investment selection for my account. I acknowledge that the Custodian has not provided or assumed responsibility for any tax, legal, structuring or investment advice with respect to this investment, and I agree that the Custodian will not be liable for any loss that results from my decision to purchase this investment. I understand that the Custodian has not reviewed nor will review the merits, legitimacy, appropriateness or suitability of this investment for my account, and I certify that I have done my own due diligence investigation prior to instructing the Custodian to make this investment for my account. I understand that the Custodian does not determine whether this investment is acceptable under the Employee Retirement Income Security Act (ERISA), the Internal Revenue Code (IRC), or any applicable federal, state, or local laws, including securities laws. I understand that it is my responsibility to review any investments to ensure compliance with these requirements.

I understand that in processing this transaction the Custodian is only acting as my agent, and nothing will be construed as conferring fiduciary status on the Custodian. I agree that the Custodian will not be liable for any investment losses sustained by me or my account as a result of this transaction. I agree to indemnify and hold harmless the Custodian from any and all claims, damages, liability, actions, costs, expenses (including reasonable attorneys' fees) and any loss to my account as a result of any action taken in connection with this investment transaction or as a result of serving as the Custodian for this investment, including, without limitation, claims, damages, liability, actions and losses asserted by me.

I understand that if this Direction of Investment and any accompanying documentation are insufficient, or if the Custodian deems it to be administratively infeasible to act as the Custodian for this investment, the Custodian may choose not to process this transaction. For instance, if the required information or documents are not received as required, or, if received, are unclear in the opinion of the Custodian; or, if there is insufficient Undirected Cash in my account to fully comply with my instructions to purchase the investment and to pay all fees. Again, the Custodian reserves the right to not process this transaction until proper documentation and/or clarification is received, and the Custodian will have no liability for loss of income or appreciation.

According to my Custodial Agreement, I understand that the Custodian, in lieu of the original records, may cause any, or all, of its records, and records at any time in its custody, to be photographed or otherwise reproduced to permanent form, and any such photograph or reproduction shall have the same force and effect as the original thereof and may be admitted in evidence equally with the original.

I understand that my account is subject to the provisions of Internal Revenue Code (IRC) §4975, which defines certain prohibited transactions. I acknowledge that the Custodian has not made nor will make any determination as to whether this investment is prohibited under §4975 or under any other federal, state or local law. I certify that making this investment will not constitute a prohibited transaction and that it complies with all applicable federal, state, and local laws, regulations and requirements.

I understand that my account is subject to the provisions of IRC §§511-514 relating to Unrelated Business Taxable Income (UBTI) of tax-exempt organizations. If this investment generates UBTI, I understand that I will be responsible for preparing or having prepared the required IRS Form 990-T tax return and any other documents that may be required. I understand that the Custodian does not make any determination of whether or not investments in my account generate UBTI.

I understand that with some types of accounts there are rules for Required Minimum Distributions (RMDs) from the account. If my account is now subject to the RMD rules, it will become subject to those RMD rules during the term of this investment, I have verified that this investment will provide income or distributions sufficient to cover each RMD; or as an alternative, I affirm that there are other liquid assets in this account or in another account from which I will be able to withdraw my RMDs. I understand that failure to take RMDs may result in a tax penalty of 50% of the amount I should have withdrawn.

I understand that all communication regarding this transaction must be in writing and must be signed by me or by my authorized agent on my behalf, and that no oral modification of my instructions will be valid. I agree to indemnify and hold harmless the Custodian and its respective officers, directors, shareholders and employees against any liability associated with making this investment, including any liability that arises because the investment is or may be a prohibited transaction under IRC §4975. I understand that I am responsible for confirming that no "disqualified person" with respect to my account will benefit from this investment in any way which is prohibited by IRC §4975.

I represent that I have done my own due diligence on the investment. I understand that the Custodian does not make any attempt to evaluate the investment or the individuals involved with the investment. I understand that I am solely responsible for evaluating the investment and its potential for profitability.

I understand that the Custodian does not bear or assume any responsibility to notify me or to secure or maintain any fire, casualty, liability or other insurance coverage, including but not limited to title insurance coverage, on this investment or on any property which serves as collateral for this investment. I acknowledge and agree that it is my sole responsibility to decide what insurance is necessary or appropriate for investments in my account, and to direct the Custodian in writing (on a form prescribed by the Custodian) to pay the premiums for any such insurance.

I further understand and agree that the Custodian is not responsible for notification or payments of any real estate taxes, homeowner's association dues, utilities or other charges with respect to this investment unless I specifically direct the Custodian to pay these amounts in writing (on a form prescribed by the Custodian), and sufficient funds are available to pay these amounts from my account. I acknowledge that it is my responsibility to provide to the Custodian or to ensure that the Custodian has received any and all bills for insurance, taxes, homeowner's dues, utilities or other amounts due for this investment. Furthermore, I agree that it is my responsibility to determine that payments have been made by reviewing my account statements.

I understand that no person at the office of the Custodian has the authority to modify any of the foregoing provisions. I certify that I have examined this Direction of Investment and any accompanying documents or information, and to the best of my knowledge and belief, it is all true, correct and complete.

Prepared By:

○ Account Holder
○ Limited Power of Attorney

_____   Signature

_____   Date

SPECIAL BONUS GIFT

CONGRATULATIONS FOR PURCHASING THIS BOOK and starting on your journey to raise MILLIONS of dollars in private money! As my way of saying thank you for taking an active role in your success education, I am gifting you and a guest access to my Private Money Academy Conference worth $2,995 per ticket! These are yours absolutely free for picking up my **Where to Get the Money Now** book!

When you attend my 3 Day Private Money Academy Conference, you'll:

- Get To Network With My Private Lenders!
- Discover The 10 Crucial Factors That Determine How Successful You Will Be.
- How To Use My 52 Secrets And Powerful Tips That Reveal How To Get More Private Money Than You Can Spend!
- Meet My "Dream Team" Including My Realtor, My Interior Designer, My Contractors, And Even My Real Estate Attorney!
- Learn How To Find Your Own Dream Team!
- Jump On A Luxury Coach Bus And See My Rehab Projects, What I'm Doing With Them, And How I'm Selling Them. Learn How To Do Business My Way… The Jay Way!
- And Much, Much More!

Simply go to https://www.JayConner.com/Conference and get registered for free today!

I've waived the $2,995 fee for both you and a guest! You can now attend for only a $97 registration fee! Or, upgrade to VIP for only $297 for you and $200 for your guest. That's almost a $6,000 savings!

Get registered here: https://www.JayConner.com/Conference

But wait!!! There's more! Get a special discount off of my **Where to Get the Money Now** system! This program retails for $2,495. Visit this special book link, and you'll get a huge discount along with several additional bonuses!

Get the WTGMN System here: https://www.JayConner.com/System

Thank you and enjoy reading!

ABOUT THE AUTHOR

J AY CONNER HAS BEEN BUYING and selling houses for over 14 years in a population of only 40,000 with profits averaging $64,000, but it wasn't always sunshine and rainbows. When the economic crash occurred around 2008, the banks cut off his funding and left him with properties under contract and no funding in site. To save his business, he knew he had to find another way.

He started searching for a new way to raise money and fund his deals. After some searching, training, and experimentation, his **Where to Get the Money Now** system was born. Using this system, Jay went on to raise $2,150,000 in less than 90 Days in Private Money and the rest is history.

Since then he has rehabbed over 400 houses and been involved in over 52 Million Dollars in transactions. He has completely automated his 7-Figure Income Business to where he works less than 10 hours per week.

He is also a leading expert on Private Lending, marketing, and business development having consulted with over 2,000 Real Estate Investors one-on-one and taught thousands more as a national speaker and trainer.

He has authored other books including his best-selling The New Masters of Real Estate: Getting Deals Done in the New Economy about real estate strategies and his currently released Private Money And You: What Is It? How To Get It? And Why You Don't Have It.

He and his wife, Carol Joy, reside in Morehead City, NC. and look forward to showing you how to raise millions of dollars in Private Money without ever asking for it and never have to depend upon banks again.